A GUIDE TO EXCELLENT (AND SUCCESSFUL) AGING

Mark H. Friedman

Owner, MBA,
Certified Dementia Practitioner
Senior Helpers Boston & South Shore

www.Guide4Aging.com

This book is meant to be a general guide based on the experiences of its author as a homecare agency owner and family caregiver. Each person's journey in aging is unique. Information provided in this book is not meant to represent specific instruction.

TABLE OF CONTENTS

FOREWORD

The first time I met Mark Friedman, I knew he was a man with a singular mission—determined to set a new standard of excellence in the senior care industry. And within a short period of time, I have seen him do this.

Mark's passion and enthusiasm for ensuring that our seniors remain safe at home, even in the face of a shrinking pool of caregivers and a burgeoning senior population, is not only admirable, it's inspiring.

While his professional background is impressive—a successful entrepreneur, an accomplished business leader, a fierce advocate for home care licensing and standardized practices in Massachusetts—it's his heart that sets him apart in the world of senior home care. Mark "gets it" when it comes to understanding the nuances of the powerful yet delicate dynamic between the caregiver and the cared for, because he's living it. As the son of parents now in their 80s, Mark is intimately involved in their lives as they age in place on their own terms, along with a little help from their sons and daughter. He's on the frontline of the effort to help seniors live out their lives at home from both personal and professional perspectives. I have observed that Mark embodies a combination of the rare qualities successful caregivers possess—passion, compassion, and expertise. And, Mark has surrounded himself with a wonderful team of professionals, who share these qualities, at Senior Helpers.

Several years ago, my partner Tom Foye and I were lucky enough to add Mark as a writer for our monthly publication, the *South Shore Senior News*. His insightful take on the business of senior home care immediately attracted the attention of our readers as Mark presents compelling, thoughtful and thought-provoking information that is cutting-edge in the senior home care profession. His columns are a hit with our audience, as readers appreciate that the critical issues surrounding aging and senior care are put in sharp focus.

I am thrilled that Mark has published this work, as it is much needed in today's complex and ever changing senior home care industry. Keep this book close at hand, as you will refer to it time and time again for the wealth of practical and insightful information it holds. You will be inspired to integrate many of Mark's best practices into your own personal and professional life. It's time we set a higher standard of excellence in senior home care. Mark Friedman's example will help get you there.

Patricia Abbate

South Shore Senior News

INTRODUCTION

Why Write This Book

Life as a Home Care Agency owner was never intended to be my career. I actually spent my first 25-plus years as a management consultant working with large practices and as a sole practitioner focused on business turnarounds, both strategic and operational. My goal was to help global companies gain viability, be successful and rise to excellence. It was a very rewarding career and I developed an expertise in diagnosing major business problems by crafting and/or navigating forces of disruption, applying leading edge management tools, and working with some of their authors. I had the opportunity to lead organizations through small, large and huge transformational changes. But along the journey I took a couple of detours.

The most significant detour was getting involved in my local synagogue. Along with a committed membership and board, I guided the consolidation of two synagogues and proceeded to lead the combined congregation in its first few years.

My wife and I were transplants to the area, with no local family, and therefore the synagogue soon became our family. Getting involved brought me closer to families of all ages and in particular with seniors. I witnessed that their connection to our community was more than just a critical part of their lives – it was woven into the fabric of their identity. Over my tenure of leadership I heard about their fears about aging, while at the same time celebrating special life moments with them, learning the histories of these remarkable people and, sadly, attending many funerals and making many calls I never wanted to make to families in mourning.

But throughout this remarkable time, I also listened intently to the impact aging had on these wonderful individuals and the challenges it brought to so many. I learned about the multi-generational impact of this journey and about the very real financial tradeoffs aging can present as funds become scarce. I learned about loneliness, about the role of community, and how poor advice from well-intentioned people can send people spiraling off course.

Enter Senior Helpers

The experience of being around an older population spoke to me in volumes that could not be ignored. It told me elder care was a critical need and one in which I should utilize the business skills I had honed over the years. I made the decision to invest in this area and began my journey, first with a partner and then on my own. As a result, the past 10-plus years have been a remarkable learning opportunity. My business background has come in handy, allowing me to diagnose the challenges of our aging population, the impact on the family structure and for those with no family, and how to navigate the confusing structure of working at the intersection of the healthcare, legal and non-medical support systems. In truth, I came to the realization that the business side of this industry is a mess. As a result, I have sought to do four things:

- To build the best Home Care Agency designed to help people age in place successfully.
- To share what I have learned by teaching professionals, guiding families and helping shape the franchise system to which I belong.
- To solve the toughest problems of aging for which Home Care is designed and to do so by setting the bar high, being uncompromising in the standard of care, and refusing to be limited by "how things have always been done."
- To challenge the flawed nature of the industry by doing things better.

I believe my agency has been successful and for that I owe deep appreciation to my excellent team who share my vision and my passion.

I am a caregiver from a distance, watching and participating in my parent's process of aging from over 600 miles away. They are the adorable couple on the cover of this book, and I owe them more then I can ever repay for instilling in me the drive to make a difference and to do so with honor and integrity.

They are our North Star in all we do at the agency. Our standard is simple: "If we wouldn't do it for our parents, Then we won't do it for yours. If we would demand it for our parents, then you can be sure that we would demand it for yours."

This book is dedicated to my family who have put up with my journey. To my parents for a life of love, mentoring and teaching. To my in-laws for their unwavering support. To my wife for making me a better man. And to my children, Lee and Dora, for inspiring me to leave good footprints on the world. Lastly, to my team, who share the task of holding our standard of excellence high and for their unwavering commitment to our clients. Their trust in me to provide a home and a platform for them professionally is a very important role for me.

Thank you.

Mark Friedman

CHAPTER ONE

Navigating the Continuum: A Case for Patience and Persistence

What makes aging in place so challenging? Is it the evolving marketplace of options, the changing rules and regulations, the confusing jargon and terminology?

Current facts and possible decision pathways provide different ways in which you can determine your own journey. What if home is *not* the right place to age in place? And if it *is,* how do you make it work on multiple dimensions?

Today your options are bolder, deeper and richer than ever. And, therefore, so must be your insights in order to make good decisions. It starts and ends with being patient, persistent, and having a plan. This means being able to navigate a landscape that will continue to do one thing: change.

The Art, Science, Patience and Persistence Required to Navigate the Continuum of Care

My company is primarily in the business of keeping seniors safe at home, designed with the intent of giving comfort to those wishing to age in place. As we age, we all see the need for companionship and hands on (personal) care to guide us through a myriad of diseases and afflictions, from post hospital, to rehab, including Recovery Care, Parkinson's, Alzheimer's, dementia and diabetes.

Home Care is not something most people casually shop for. In my field there is a common saying: "You don't know what you need until AFTER you know you need it." Yes, identifying the need for support is tangled, but families know exactly what I am referring to.

Ninety percent of seniors know they want to stay in their own homes, but don't know quite how to put all the pieces together to make it happen. This alone can cause enormous anxiety, especially when complicated by health issues, both real or anticipated. This can often become a family challenge as each member may have a different idea of what "good" looks like, or what words like "aging successfully" or "being happy later in life," really mean.

Home Care is all about delivering care and the corresponding peace of mind to seniors and their loved ones. Seniors need a trustworthy advocate to help them navigate the muddy waters of current situations by helping them connect to this peace of mind. The goal is to help alleviate anxieties and the impact on families by supporting family caregivers and by defining needs around the house for personal care, companionship and other activities.

The "care world" is being redefined every day in consequential ways. The language is getting more complicated, the players in it more difficult to discern. The costs are skyrocketing and no one is immune to the toll caregiving is taking on the family wallet and the level of stress it puts on everyone. In addition, times have changed. The fact is, adult children are no longer naturally expected or inclined to take care of aging parents, and the landscape of caregiving is adjusting to this evolution in attitude and a shift in responsibilities.

The need for support create tender times for seniors and is nothing to be cavalier about. Because decisions about aging can be heart-wrenching and transitions are complicated, finding the right "next" and often last home can be extraordinarily daunting.

You need to prepare for a successful journey of aging in place by anticipating the challenges ahead, preparing for them in an intelligent fashion, and being able to make important decisions along the way. Yes, there is a process involved. And this should make many seniors very happy, especially those who like to be in control and find the process of discovery energizing. Planning for a journey of aging requires diligence and should not be left to whimsy or chance. Think of it as planning a great road trip!

Home Care agencies work with families and seniors to help them make home the best and safest place to age, or to help transition them from a traditional "Home" setting by minimizing stress and maximizing the ability to make informed decisions every step of the way. In subsequent chapters we reveal why home care is becoming the most desired option for recovery care and aging in place as we begin to master ways to make it safe and compelling for both, due to extraordinary caregivers, caregiver recruitment, training and skills education, and the impact of technology.

A fully integrated Home Care Agency will help families frame what is important and leverage substantial relationships and connections in the community on their behalf. This is easy to do when we keep the senior and family the center of the discussion, and by recognizing that each senior will journey differently through the aging process.

The real point here is this: understanding the continuum of care enables you to develop a plan as a powerful first step. Because in the absence of a plan, all roads get you nowhere.

In 2012 "Next Avenue" marched onto the senior living scene as the digital PBS for the older generation. Its mission, "where grown-ups keep growing," is bold; as it unleashed the potential of elders through the power of robust media. It boasts that 95% of its "members" take action after reading its stories online on various platforms or because of its partnerships. "Next Avenue" believes in recycling great ideas; what was once new and attention-grabbing is always worth refreshing.

It is a reminder to all of us working with seniors that we should never get tired of explaining what matters, especially if what matters is important.

A recent headline gave me pause: "Will Your Home Be Ready for Aging in Place?" It reminds me of a larger question I am asked every day as owner of a home care agency: "What do I need to do to age in place?"

When so many seniors wish to age in place, this question is always timely and bears asking, answering, and asking again (and again). Seniors and loved ones will address scores of common issues, which in turn require patience, persistence, and highly personalized plans that need to adapt as we age. Why? Because most seniors will be navigating a similar continuum of care that will always be evolving. Yet, no two will experience the same journey of aging.

To Build a Plan, You Must Know Your Options

Navigating the Continuum: Studies show few people are prepared for the challenges and unpredictability of managing their own care or the care of a parent or loved one. Seniors did not expect to live this long. Medical and social needs of the now rapidly "growing Oldest-Old" are more complicated. Costs of care are much more than anticipated. Assumptions about who would take care of seniors continue to change. The eldercare continuum is a fog of players, made more confusing by Google and search engines in general. Housing options, "Home," and models of care are constantly evolving. Too often we get well-meaning advice from the wrong professionals. The world of seniors has splintered into sub-specialists who are equipped to provide highly personalized guidance, from experts within the Aging Life Care Association, to legal counsel from the National Academy of Elder Law Attorneys (NAELA). Navigating this world is indeed possible, especially if you're not in crisis-mode while trying to do so.

Addressing Health and Abilities to Function: Warning signs that help may be needed include a myriad of physical, emotional and cognitive issues, and we usually wait too long to address them. These include everything from chronic health problems (diabetes, COPD, heart disease), to occasional issues with trouble walking, falls, and an inability to perform activities of daily living, such as dressing. Often, we overlook signs of depression, social withdrawal, confusion, medication mix-up and financial problems.

The navigational challenge begins by honestly sorting out care across four critical dimensions and asking:

- What type of care do I require now, and potentially in the future?
- Where will I live?
- What will it cost?
- What resources can I access or harness?

While home might be the most desired option, these days it is no longer the only option. It has many extended definitions including independent and assisted living communities, 65-plus rental housing complexes, CCRC's and innovative and inventive congregant homes. For those not familiar with the term, a CCRC is a Continuing Care Retirement Community (CCRC), also known as a life plan community. It's the type of U.S. retirement community where a continuum of aging care needs—from independent living, assisted living, and skilled nursing care—can all be met within the community. These various levels of shelter and care may be housed on different floors or wings of a single high-rise building or in physically adjacent buildings, such as garden apartments, cottages, duplexes, mid-and low-rise buildings, or spread out in a campus setting. The emphasis of the CCRC model is to enable residents to avoid having to move, except to another level of care within the community, if their needs change.

In creating your plan, your Circle-of-Care is your essential support system. In addition to family members and medical professionals and professional caregivers, the Circle-of-Care may include nutrition and nutritionists, therapy and therapists, medications and medical disciplines, exercise and exercise routines. This is your bullpen, safety net, and go-to team. It may change over time with professionals moving in and out, and at times include legal and tax counsel, financial advisors, and support from community resources. The point here is your "Circle" is personal, fluid, and requires updating and renewal as you move through your journey or supporting a loved one through theirs.

Consider these questions when deciding who to include in yours:

- What role does each person play and why?
- Who are the experts and who are the "friends"?
- Have I covered my bases? Medically? Legally? Financially? Geographically? Emotionally?
- What are the important documents I require? Are they

updated and who should have ownership of them? (Power of Attorney, Living Wills, etc.)

"The single biggest problem in communication is the illusion that it has taken place." --George Bernard Shaw

One might think that through the combination of the healthcare system and the power of the Internet we would have an unparalleled communications superhighway. Well, not quite.

Today, we can look up any specialist in the world on LinkedIn or a hospital website. We can check his or her background, years in his or her field, degrees and pedigree. We can search procedures, drug interactions and diagnoses for thousands of ailments on WebMD or scores of other sites, as well as share war stories of botched surgeries on Facebook. But is this really "taking charge" of our own care?

The concept of the Accountable Care Organization looked great in theory; synchronized care through efficiently managed partnerships. Yet its veracity is being tested every day because people are human and it takes humans to communicate, integrate, and coordinate. Some embrace the approach and some don't. But you have to be your own "general contractor" or enlist someone who will.

What has not dissipated is the continued regard for Patient-Centered Care, a concept coined back in 2007 that scores how well care meets eight important criteria; all focused on putting the patient first and foremost. The score means to answer how well patient care answers these questions:

- Do you respect my values, preferences and needs?
- Can you coordinate my care?
- Can you keep me informed *and* educated?
- Do you understand my need for physical comfort?
- Do you understand my need for emotional support to alleviate fear?
- Do you understand my need to involve family and friends?
- Can you help me with continuity and transition?
- Can you help me with access to care?

What this Patient-Centered Care concept also implies is an expressed ownership on the part of the patient of his or her own health management. If this is to be a successful way to think about care, there has to be responsibility from both parties.

In Chapter Two we will explore the implications of Patient-Centered Care further. Because, with seniors living longer, healthier lives, healthcare management will need to be a shared responsibility.

This is important for seniors to acknowledge as they plan for longer lives, especially when confronted with more complicated healthcare decisions down the road. By forming a thoughtful Circle-of-Care, they have a strong team of multi-lateral and interdisciplinary support for their deeply personal journey. Who could ask for more?

When Home Is the Preferred Option

When families choose home for aging in place my advice is always to keep it simple. It usually is quite easy to figure out what is required to establish a very smart plan of care if you know what questions to ask.

I use the story of the "OMG" visit. This is the returning home of adult children and "sandwichers" to find parents and family elders not aging well in place. For months they have been perched their respective distance from hundreds or thousands of miles away. What they hear during Sunday calls and in energetic emails is "everything is just fine," when in fact it is the opposite of what they see when they walk through the front door. Then, it's "OMG, what has happened to mom and dad?"

When loved ones start asking about neighbors, foods they know mom loves, weekly games and outings dad enjoys, they are employing intentional ways of discovering the patterns of daily lives. Do mom and dad get out of the house with frequency? Are they engaged in the community they love? Do they see long standing friends?

Through these questions a pattern of daily life will emerge; including a solid diet, energetic engagement in the world and a general contentment for being at home. More troublesome signs will also reveal themselves.

When it comes to setting up a plan of support for a parent a simple plan is usually the smartest plan; especially if it focuses on five ingredients:

- Making home a safe place to be
- Optimizing medical condition management
- Supporting autonomy and independence
- Engaging in life to the fullest
- Easing the burden of care on others to ensure everyone succeeds

We help families structure a support plan around these five ingredients for one major reason: it works. Our approach is called the LIFE Profile. It is a proprietary methodology that helps mitigate the risk factors at home that stand in the way of your success, while at the same time giving us the tools to design effective support for care. We're poised to get this end of your journey covered. We discuss more fully in Chapter Four how LIFE Profile™ works, fully exploring how decades of scientific research and thousands of trials have created a stunning approach to successful aging in place. The philosophy, methodology, and fundamental principles behind it are remarkably simple and designed for a senior's individual journey of aging. The point is that there should be a defined, well planned approach to everything you do.

This chapter started with a reference about whether or not your home is ready for aging in place. Hopefully it has given you plenty to think about in order to answer the larger questions – will you be ready?

CHAPTER TWO

Becoming An Educated Consumer: Getting Started, Taking Charge

Keeping up with the world of eldercare is like trying to hit a constantly moving target, one throwing off more complex data than the human brain can possibly absorb. To suggest we must become uber-educated when it comes to planning our own journey of aging is like tossing the map of the world in the trunk of our car and wishing ourselves a safe trip to wherever we think we're going.

My intent is to keep your journey focused on possibilities that are doable for you. Those that are limitless in possibilities yet pragmatic in execution. But it still requires you to take charge of planning the trip. So let's get started by addressing a few areas, such as:

Just how big, bold and boundless will your world be? How will you define your strategy for aging in place?

Who, how, what and where are "seniors" anyway?

I am constantly in the company of elders and families. This allows me to trade expertise with caregivers, geriatricians, medical professionals and advisors from all disciplines who provide seniors with crucial counsel. I get an up close and personal view of what is going on in the process of aging; and what causes anxiety and stress in seniors and extended family members.

I know that the term "senior" has been radically redefined in the last decade. No longer simply synonymous with the 5 o'clock dinner specials at Denny's, a "senior" can now fill out four decades of living. As they say; "80" is the new "65".

Boston Globe writer Robert Weisman regularly covers issues of interest to and for seniors, and he recently penned a front-page article entitled "In a New Age, Everyone's Getting Older But Nobody's Getting Old." His piece explains the difficulty we all have in describing a span of 40 years that used to be comfortably called "senior" or "elderly." These monikers are now met with backlash and everyone from assisted living communities to advocacy groups are grappling with life-stage nomenclature. Weisman goes on to say that durable names like 'aging' and 'seniors', still in widespread use and part of the names of countless organizations, are fast becoming radioactive. I will let others grapple with definitions and the changing vocabulary around this dynamic pool of people. But no matter the label, it does not alter the importance of thinking about your own journey of aging, or the journey of a loved one.

Think of how big, bold and boundless your world seemed when you were 16 and only beginning to imagine the next 50 years of your life. How seniors are doing today, as opposed to 50 years ago, has been dramatically reinvented with our medical, health and wellness communities stepping up their games in the transformation.

Seniors are also taking pro-active roles in their own healthcare management. They are planning their journeys of aging by becoming better informed and better educated consumers. I am heartened when seniors and families make important decisions before a crisis arises, because they know they can be robbed of important options if they do not.

Where seniors live has also been radically modified because so has the definition of "Home." Whether it is an assisted living community, an in-law apartment, or a multi-family dwelling where four childhood friends decide to age together, we appreciate the metamorphosis of "Home" within the journey of aging. This is the beauty of private duty home care; its portability.

The Power to Profile & Define a Good Day

Acclaimed surgeon and *New Yorker* columnist Atul Gawande, author of "Being Mortal," is no stranger to difficult conversations. On subjects like "Rethinking Old Age" and "The Way We Age Now," he continually challenges both the medical profession and seniors with questions like, "What is a good day?"

As a thought leader, Gawande has taught millions of us how to listen to the voices of elders in their journey of aging, and to risk more in making our days rewarding and fulfilling.

Gawande begs the question of what quality of life means to each of us. There is no reason to believe that as we age our world needs to get smaller just because we cannot do all that we used to do. It just means we can do other things, different things, bigger things. And we can do this by using our brains, our energy, our dreams, our wit and, especially, our wisdom. Just because we need support does not mean we lose autonomy and independence. It means we retain it.

The opportunity to live boundlessly lies just ahead. It is in fact the perfect time to think boundlessly about what a great day looks like, and to plan for more of them. One day at a time.

Caught In the Middle is Not the Same as Being Caught off Guard: Thoughts for My Sandwich Generation and Adult Children of all ages

I love the fact that there is a designated "National Sandwich Generation Month." It speaks to my generation, millions of adult children who for the first time are facing a parental tsunami of sorts. While busy with careers and raising families of our own, very often miles, states, and now countries away from our parents, we are also facing enormous conflicts about how to care for our aging loved ones. We all live in fear of a dreaded phone call, or perhaps one of those "OMG Visits."

Every day I get calls from an adult child about concerns for mom, dad or a loved one. The call may come in from Miami or Milan, but the anxieties are the same: Mom seems confused, she may not be eating, she hasn't left the house in days, and her friends are calling and worried. Or maybe an only uncle is going in for surgery and there are no plans for care in place when it is completed.

Then, there is the "OMG Visit." All year long the kids have been counting on vacationing on the Cape with the grandparents, but arrive only to find granddad forgetful and the house in disarray. The immediate observation is things are just "not right." These visits, which very often take place on holidays and school vacations, are frightening for the Sandwich Generation. That's why I call them the "Oh My God" visits because that's when it is shockingly apparent that mom or dad needs help, and it's time to mobilize. But mobilize what? Mobilize how?

The fact is our parents are living longer than ever and through the grace of modern medicine are managing more complex health issues along the way. We know this because a multi-billion dollar industry has ballooned to support them at home, in a variety of care communities, in robust day centers of activities, and with the help of hundreds of for-profit and not-for-profit agencies and organizations, all designed to engage them mentally, physically, and emotionally for as long as they are able.

I am part of this Sandwich Generation, which cuts a substantial swath of adults as young as 40 and as old as 70. It occurs to me that as I am out educating seniors about "Navigating the Continuum of Care," the topics and issues I share with them are absolutely relevant for these adult children. It is the Sandwich Generation that is now playing an essential part in helping parents and loved ones fulfill their wish to age in place. I know because I am one of them (the cute couple on the back cover of this book is my parents.)

The Sandwichers are becoming primary caregivers, and in this role consumers of all-things senior. Like their parents, they need to understand where to turn for help, how to think about costs associated with living and lifestyle choices, and how to be an educated consumer.

The Sandwichers as Caregivers

According to AARP, 85-90% of seniors want to remain living in their home even as their needs for assistance with Activities of Daily Living (ADL's) increase. Of elders receiving care, 85% reside in their own home, or that of a loved one.

What Does a Family Caregiver Profile Look Like?

- 44.4 million Americans (21% of the adult population) act as caregivers.
- One third act as caregivers to two or more people.
- 83% of caregivers are related to their care recipients.
- Average caregiver's age is 46 years old.
- 59% are employed.
- The primary family caregiver (usually the oldest daughter, who is also working) spends an average of 20

hours per week caring for an elderly parent.

- 1 in 5 caregivers provide over 40 hours of care.
- 40% of caregivers who work full-time report missing work on a regular basis due to the health needs of an elderly loved one.
- 54% of working caregivers say they were unprepared for schedule juggling.
- 80% of working caregivers report emotional strain.
- Caregivers are twice as likely as non-caregivers to report physical and mental health complications.
- 50% of working caregivers report financial strain from providing care for aging parents.

Sandwichers embarking on the role as primary caregiver to an aging parent or loved one are embarking on the job of their lifetime. Will they ever be fully prepared for it? Absolutely not. But today, in part because so many adult children find themselves in these roles, there are organizations that provide respite and support, training and encouragement, to this new and incredibly critical role in our aging ecosystem.

In Chapter Four we discuss the issue of "Burden of Care," which is everything that goes into the issue of "caregiving." We will tackle caregiver burnout and its telltale signs, and the importance of getting support for family caregivers that comes in the form of formal family training, general navigation, specific caregiving for Alzheimer's, dementia, Parkinson's Disease, and other critical needs on the journey of aging.

Adult children need to understand both the beauty and the enormity of their undertaking and think through what their role really means.

- How do they split time between children/family and their elder loved one?
- How much time is too much time in their care-giving role?
- How will they find time for their marriage?
- How will they find time for themselves?
- How will they find the resources they need for themselves and their loved one?
- How will they combat feelings of isolation?
- How can they handle potential guilt for not having enough time to accomplish all that they "should" be doing?
- What's the "what if" scenario and back-up game plan should things change suddenly?

Connections, Community, Customization... Creating a Surefooted Sandwich Generation

I believe the Sandwich Generation knows the enormity of what lies ahead; the importance of being informed and prepared is essential. Understanding options, access and providers is critical, but so is having a clear definition of what excellence means for us and our families.

Working to ensure the well-being of a senior requires preparation and decision-making around medical, legal, financial, geographic, and emotional issues. If you and your siblings are ready to navigate this landscape, there are resources available to support your journey. I hope you will find some of what you need within the pages of this book.

The other thing I know to be true is this: no one successfully ages alone. To do so we need each other and we need to understand the unique nature of each of our journeys. We must stress quality of life over quantity, and if we keep seniors front and center, we can accomplish this.

Every year I am reminded that October is Patient-Centered Care Month. This resonates with me because I often talk about seniors being the center of our universe, so I was more than curious as to how our approach to caregiving aligned with the "patient-centered care" model popularized in the broader healthcare system.

How do we measure up?

The term "patient-centered care" was originally coined back in 2007, a result of scores of focus groups, national telephone interviews and of patients and families that created the "Picker" survey instrument. This measured the patient's experience across eight dimensions of care, which became the Picker/Commonwealth Dimensions.

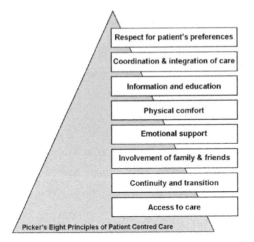

Respect for patient's preferences

Coordination & integration of care

Information and education

Physical comfort

Emotional support

Involvement of family & friends

Continuity and transition

Access to care

Picker's Eight Principles of Patient Centred Care

Once I discovered the involvement of the Commonwealth Fund in patient-centered care, I knew we all should take notice.

The Commonwealth Fund is a world class research institute and grant maker that funds both domestic and international health care surveys, as well as national, state and local health care scorecards. It follows and influences policies and politics, and contributes to developing and reforming the likes of the Affordable Care Act and covering every hiccup on the Hill during the health care debates.

It is the "go to" authority on this topic of patient care. When I began my journey in providing care for seniors, I was unaware of the specifics of Picker/Commonwealth. But now that I do I ask myself, "Do they matter?"

The question is this: If these issues are important to you, are you being well served by your medical professionals, your home care company and other care providers? This is for you to determine, which means these standards are for you to apply....or not.

Do You Respect My Values, Preferences and Expressed Needs?

This seems like such a no-brainer, but it is not.

Learning to be a great listener is often an acquired skill. Understanding cultural differences and values requires training, sensitivity, practice and openness. Often, we first meet our clients in their homes, we might spend an hour talking about favorite memories, meals, family trips and keepsakes around the living room. We do this to learn as much as we can about personal histories, priorities, and interests. The intent is to find the best match of caregivers. This is not a random pairing, but a coordinated connection: part art, part science. We know our caregivers are also life-givers and often become deep family friends and companions. We work hard to create these potential connections.

Being a good listener matters. However, being good listeners does not translate to "blind following." Most of us will, at some point, face tradeoffs between needs, desires, rights, wrongs, costs, etc. What we want may not be what we need or even be appropriate. Providers must be trusted partners in care to help you make informed choices – even the ones you may not want to make. Can they coordinate and integrate your care?

"This is *not* what I expected for mom's companion." We get that a lot.

As an increasingly viable option to support aging in place, Home Care must respond to the complex physical considerations in which many seniors find themselves. Well trained caregivers are needed for seniors in different stages of Alzheimer's, dementia and Parkinson's diseases. There are too many moving parts where these diagnoses are concerned; from coordination of diets, activities, exercise and medication regimens, to engaging family support. These require foresight and insight, a thoughtful approach to care management, and above all, a philosophy of care that is dynamic and inclusive.

Can You Keep Me Informed and Educated?

"The single biggest problem in communication is the illusion that it has taken place."
George Bernard Shaw

You would think in this information age the healthcare system would have an unparalleled communications superhighway. Well, not quite. While the concept of the Accountable Care Organization looked great in theory, it is being tested every day because people are human and it takes humans to communicate, integrate, and coordinate. We referenced this notion in Chapter One, but we mention it again because it is important to understand that care "management" is a joint custody issue that must be managed by the professionals and co-owned by us as consumers. Here is where information and education must work together.

As an example, our "Going Home Safe" program is a multi-dimensional program allowing seniors to recover safely at home by coordinating communications and responsibilities among the chain of providers to manage the risks that can result in readmission. We understand that discharge really starts at admission, when important decisions about recovery are being made while a senior is in the hospital. Because without comfort, *there is no care.*

A sense of well being gives seniors their best days. We understand this comfort means being able to do the most they are capable of doing, from simple acts such as bathing, dressing and cooking, to things they simply enjoy doing. The ability to experience the small and big activities that make them happy is what's important.

There is an old saying that goes: "You don't know what you need until *after* you know you need it."

Seniors know they want to stay in their own homes, but don't know quite how to put all the pieces together. This alone can cause enormous anxiety, especially when complicated by health issues. This can often become a family challenge as each member may have a different idea of what "good" looks like. The eldercare industry needs to do more than just deliver care. It has to deliver expertise that corresponds to peace of mind. This means helping seniors take control of their current situations, connect them to new resources, define needs that others haven't quite yet identified, and support extended family caregivers. It's doing more than what is asked and required. Simply put, being good at one thing is no longer good enough.

To Help Seniors Age in Place at Home it Usually Takes a Village

In the Senior Living industry, it is essential to have deep and rich connections to "all things senior." It is important to be entrenched in the communities and recognize the value that outside relationships bring into the home. Engaging in life is critical to aging successfully in place. Getting transportation and support for social and religious activities, doctor's appointments, luncheons and the all-important social engagements are critical, and should include the involvement of friends and family.

Can You Help Me with Continuity and Transition?

In the Picker/Commonwealth Study, the concerns around continuity and transition after discharge loom large. There are intense anxieties around medications, physical limitations, dietary needs, coordination of treatments, access to information going forward and future clinical, social and physical support.

The biggest issue for patients is access to care. Is Washington listening? This is where we all must do our very best to ensure that seniors have access to hospitals, clinics and physician offices. We must be drivers, and make transportation available, help make appointments easy to schedule and change – without penalties. We must make referrals understandable and obtainable, with clear and simplified instructions attached. But we must also realize that we are just one cog in a very large wheel.

Today, measuring up simply is not good enough as we continue to see 90% of seniors choosing to remain at home, while expecting us to do better at helping them age successfully while there. Millions will need our collective efforts helping them stay safe, engaged in life, independent, autonomous and comfortable.

CHAPTER THREE

Prepare to Succeed: Critical Elements of a Great Plan

A plan for success defines the What, the Why, and the Who, and will be part of your Journey of Aging. In previous chapters we started to define your "baseline," the issues now baked into your current and foreseeable future. It's time to define your broader "Circle-of-Care" – because it will respond to change, and those in it will help you manage uncertainty successfully. As you gain courage, commitment and command of the facts, your plan takes shape with increasing confidence.

When the Hardest Advice to Give is Your Own

Home Care agencies routinely work with families – adult children of seniors, and the seniors themselves, in forming and reconciling their checklist for aging in place successfully. The "place" is wherever they designate, and "Home" has many definitions. I am fully aware how difficult this process can be and how long the "checklist" can look. I have witnessed how complicated it is for families to define an action plan for a loved one and to clarify who does what. I also have had to apply all I have learned to help my own loved ones "have the conversation."

A Personal Story That Goes Something Like This

I had the opportunity to visit my parents in southern Virginia. They are the adorable, radiant couple on the cover of my agency brochure. I am truly blessed. They are amazing individuals and an amazing couple. They are in their early-80's and are very successfully aging in place at home. Yes, they have their typical health events, but all are self-managed and well-managed. Like many seniors, they do not have adult children living close by but are surrounded by lifelong friends and extended family. My sister, brother and I agree that our only desire is that our folks age on their own terms, and that all of their resources be dedicated entirely to that one goal. Most importantly, we are lucky in that as a family we trust and respect each other. But even an expert has apprehensions.

As I was getting ready for my visit, I looked at the list of questions we customarily ask families about their aging in place process. I quickly realized that as a family we could not begin to clearly answer all of them. As I rehearsed in my head the discussion for my visit, it hit me that ideally my brother, sister and I should all be together for this "talk." I did not plan as well as I could have, but I had prepared. I used my acquired expertise to write out a set of questions and previewed the questions with my folks. I had made it crystal clear that my only goal was to help him get what they want. Yet I was still nervous about how the conversation would go.

The Value of Ah-Ha Moments

What struck me before getting on the plane to Virginia was although I had played a valuable role in helping my clients define their criteria for successful aging, my siblings and I were clearly not role models in coordinating conversations like the ones I was about to have with our parents. Questions kept going through my head:

- How could we know how to help them get what they wanted when we didn't know what those things were?
- What are the tradeoffs they are or are not willing to make?
- What documentation do I need to complete, and where are the critical documents we need to assemble?
- Is planning for Medicaid something to be considered or not? If not, how does that impact future decisions?
- If my siblings and I need to make decisions, who was going to make them?
- How would the expected differences of opinion be reconciled?
- Who would be the "lead" for different types of decisions?

The list went on and on. It was part of very rational, orderly plan; easy to write out, read, categorize and advise others about. The fact is, my parents had thought out most of them, but at a high level. With changes in tax laws, medical (Medicare and Medicaid) insurance qualification rules and other systemic changes in our healthcare system, it was now essential to review documents carefully, beginning with knowing where these critical documents are located.

During these initial conversations I came to appreciate my parent's experiences and biases towards different types of financial planning and advice tools. We had emotional discussions about control and decision-making when looking at autonomy and independence strategies and trade-offs.

Expect the Unexpected

I knew this particular weekend with my parents would be emotionally charged, but I was unprepared for just how much so. These few days were the beginning of a longer set of conversations we will all continue to have. I thought I would share my reconciled map of how I see these complicated, critical yet difficult dialogues. Because that is exactly what these are; powerful communications that can significantly impact the ability of loved ones to age successfully.

Have the Conversations Before There is a Crisis – Do Not Wait

Do not go in with answers; go in with a set of questions. You do not, cannot, nor will you ever be able to comprehend what the world looks like from another person's perspective. Even if that person is your mother, father, best friend, partner, or longest living loved one. Ask questions, listen with intention, learn with eagerness, and think positively. Take notes!

This is a process that will set the stage for a loved one aging successfully: a "set" of discussions, a continuous and ongoing dialogue. It is not a "one and done" conversation. Be patient but at the same time be persistent.

Be respectful not authoritative. There is no right or wrong answer that works for everyone. Answers must fit the priorities and perspective of your parents or loved one – NOT YOURS. Make sure to reassure them that they are in control.

Be Transparent: There cannot be hidden agendas either with your parents or siblings (or others involved). Creating an atmosphere of trust and transparency may require some negotiations and even outside perspectives. Be open to this.

Be clear – this is not about taking control. This is about what you can do to help loved ones define and achieve the highest level of priorities they set for themselves. Together create a plan for next steps: Support your loved one's decision regarding getting outside expertise for help. Even if you have the specific skills to do things yourself (financial advice, legal advice, etc.), this may not be the right role for you in this particular context. Schedule future conversations. Keep this dialogue going and determine who in the family and extended circle needs to be part of them going forward.

Treasure the Times

As I replayed this first visit with my folks, I was grateful to rely on substance I had learned as the owner of a Home Care agency. I realized I had acquired deep insights from powerful resources. Before my visit I had referred back to copious notes I have from hours of conversations with professionals in elder law, elder care management, financial and Medicaid planning, and things I have learned from organizations such as Honoring Choices. The fact is I had a tremendous leg up in our conversations, but it didn't make me any less apprehensive as to how my visit would ultimately turn out.

While boarding the plane back to Boston, I recognized, however, we had triumphed as a family. We had started the conversation, asked the questions, listened well and respectfully. We had begun to empower a plan together.

What a treasure this particular weekend was for me as a son. I still learn from you, Mom and Dad. Thank you - you have again helped me grow personally and as a professional.

Stability in the Face of Uncertainty

When our stability is at risk, we all are fearful. For seniors, this can be particularly unsettling. Emotions run the gamut from who's is to blame, when will stability be regained, why did it happen, and is it my fault? What can I do to prevent it from happening again? I can't go on, should I give up? These mixed emotions make navigating the process of aging even more complex. The source can be economic, weather, family, public assistance and a myriad of "other."

In uncertain times, seniors worry. Accurate or not, they are concerned over Social Security, Medicare payments and more. They cut back on care and miss important appointments. Meaningful activities and engagements seniors need and feel deeply about can be suddenly thrown out of whack. These are not incidental pursuits for elders, but essential to quality of life. Unsettling times highlight the role a home care agency plays in being a source of certainty and confidence for seniors – as do all providers. We have to adapt to changing conditions and learn from each "disruption" to better support them during these periods.

The Confidence of Preparation

Being truly *prepared* comes not from a big "ah ha" moment, but the confidence from executing and knowing how to tweak meticulously developed care plans. We use a proprietary approach, the LIFE Profile™. This is an assessment methodology that focuses on identifying risk factors which can create instability with regard to aging in place. This includes:

- Safety (144 potential risk factors)
- Medical Condition Management (seven critical needs)
- Autonomy and Independence (13 basic needs we have to meet)

- Burden of Care on others
- Quality of life engagement

As the comfortable footings of seniors seemed to shift, this is the basis for a sturdy road map to follow and a reassuring message to deliver to those in our care – it translates to a care plan designed to mitigate those risk factors. The plan tells us what care is needed, why that care is needed, and then defines roles and responsibilities within the person's Circle-of-Care (i.e. family, friends, professional caregivers, case managers and medical professionals).

When clients have a defined and focused approach to care and support, they are teed up for success, creating an even greater source of stability and probability of success. It gives us, as a professional partner the detailed view to manage whether, outside circumstances posing potential threats, essential needs, and points of risk across all five critical success factors for successful aging.

With Science Behind it, an Arsenal of Data to Support Good Sense

Data showing 144 potential safety risks can undermine success at home, therefore it makes sense to inventory the environment of elders. When there is a clear understanding of what "Home" looks like and how a senior manages and maneuvers within it, we can craft a plan in concert with the individuals Circle-of-Care to mitigate and/or remove the risks altogether.

One thing that drives anxiety at warp speed with adult children concerned for parents living on their own is managing medications. As seniors age and face more complex diagnoses, compliance to treatments, appointments and medication regimes become more complicated and more critical. Yes, 24/7 access to experienced doctors and consultations, provided with the push of a button are now emerging. But, the more basic issues of can I get my medications, can I figure out my dosage, can I take them as prescribed, can I document my compliance and if I am monitoring my vitals, can I log them and know what to do if they fall out of my target range(s). A care plan should define and provide documentation for all of this.

Turning fear into fearlessness. Whether 77 or 97, seniors passionately want to hold on to basic activities associated with autonomy and independence. We take most of these for granted; bill paying, grocery shopping, meal planning and prep, laundry and trash. Many seniors feel threatened at the prospect of losing control of the tasks they consider essential to their independence.

Customized plans of care identify which tasks may require additional bracing for any unforeseen circumstance. A focused deployment of resources can then pick up the slack while advocating the broadest boundaries of autonomy and independence that seniors' desire. It is surprisingly easy to revisit plans of care and double down on resources in strategic ways during fractious and uncertain times because the solid grounding is already in place.

Living large when days seem small. Uncertainty often leads to "hunkering down." Near zero-degree weather can shut people off from engaging in life, even if temporarily. When seniors are "engaged" in activities that matter to them they simply live happier and more fulfilling lives. This "engagement" is different for every senior because their conversations about quality of life differ depending on age, desire, circumstances of health and other variables. Protecting the lives of seniors from becoming "smaller," and as a result more stressful, is a key by-product of good home care.

Quality of life engagement is critical. Good plans for care include support for active life engagement. Think of it as creating a giant game board with interchangeable pieces. Even with an unplanned shut-in due to extreme weather, the meaning behind the engagements on that board are fully understood. A long-planned trip to the museum can be pushed to a later date and replaced with a comparable activity. Other events can be shifted around. Helping to arrange and re-arrange the pieces on the game board, establishing and making alternative plans happen, is always possible when you know what is important. For seniors and families, it means that home care support can be pragmatic, practical, and always fluid.

The key is this: The assessment and care plan must be comprehensive. By this I mean it cannot be limited to the care being provided by an agency or others. It has detail and substance, not just a series of check boxes. The care plan is about the individual, 24/7, all 168 hours of a week. The second step is to document who does what and the third step is to define how it should be done. Well defined assessments that drive a comprehensive care plan like this enable the individual's total "system" of care (professionals, family, friends and self) to manage a 360° view of risk. The result is a pragmatic, practical, confident orchestration of care.

Navigating "Home" in Uncertain Times

In a macro-sense, periods of acute uncertainty test the resiliency of a plan. We must navigate with our eyes on many details and have contingency plans within easy reach. "Home" must be more than just viable, it must be a platform for stability especially if it is to be the place seniors most want to continue their journey of aging.

Here are three helpful tips for you as you navigate or advise others in the journey of aging:

- Understand the risks for aging in place. The end-result should be a strategically focused care plan and system for care in which tradeoffs can be made with full information.
- Make every dollar count. Resources deployed for managing the right risks for the right reasons make it possible to avoid potential potholes on your journey – big ones, permanent ones and temporary ones. It ensures

that every dollar invested in home care works harder, smarter and longer to keep you safe secure, engaged and successful.

- Make sure your risk assessment and plan of care have "what-if" components. These could include short-term weather or longer-term changing economic or medical resources. Make sure providers have contingency plans. Will they guarantee services? How do they stand behind them operationally? Up front discussions on these concerns are very reasonable conversations to have. There is no doubt, with plans and preparations, the journey of aging can weather the unpredictable.

I have seen so many people struggling to do this; some who were champions of the journey and too many who were victims whose journeys could have been so much better. I have seen amazing people stopped in place because they got bad advice, the wrong advice, or were simply not prepared for the decisions, and the planned and unplanned life events that were on their journey to age in place. I have seen families torn apart at the seams by this journey, as well as families come together like high powered magnets.

Here are several key things you need to know to help you plan your journey. Nothing comes together by accident. Excellent planning is always required, and it is never too early to start or too late. Few people do complete planning, yet most think they did not only *complete* planning but also *excellent* planning. It is rare that I have ever seen complete or excellent planning.

Plans are old: They no longer reflect the individual's current reality, their objectives or their needs. If your plans are two to five years old–redo them, or at least review them. Plans are based on impossible expectations; we assume the best in our planning.

Do some scenario planning: What will you do if or when:

- Rules change
- Tax Laws change
- Medicaid Qualification Rules change
- Medicare changes
- Readmission penalties of the ACA changes

People confuse wants with needs. Are you clear about the difference between them in your case? Are you absolutely sure about this? People fail to set priorities before planning. Define what tradeoffs you are willing to make. Are you sure about them?

Recommendation: Review your plans. Be clear about how you are going to receive the right information about changing regulations that will impact your decisions now and in the future.

Form your own "Advisory Board" because your decisions should not be made in a vacuum and you need the right team around you. Communicate your intent, your status, your priorities, your willingness for tradeoffs, and how you want decisions made with your network of care providers and loved ones. Put it in writing and revisit regularly. My advice is to start a notebook and evolve your thoughts in it. Share it and do not be afraid to change your thinking along the way. Make sure it includes:

- Doctors & specialists
- Lawyers
- Financial Planners
- Family & extended loved ones
- If available, aging service providers you use

Recommendation: Have a formal sit-down with your providers (professional, family, friends, etc) so individuals know what you're thinking. Get feedback. Ask honest questions as to whether they can play the role you are asking and find out if they are cast in the proper role and have the time, resources and, most importantly, the expertise to play the role you have cast them in.

Get professional advice from the right professionals. Too often, people get advice from the wrong people. Or get incomplete advice. People confuse tax planning with *care planning* and/or *financial planning* with a money professional. Understand what a reputable provider is; and know what "good" means.

Know the credentialing standards/Standards of Excellence

- Elder Law: NAELA
- Financial Planner: CFP

- Medical: Geriatrician
- Care Management: GCM, now "Aging Life Care Professional"
- Home Care: Understand the difference between an Agency versus a Registry model, and the implications of hiring caregivers "Under the table" (more on this in Chapter 4)

Remember, people get bad advice from good and well-meaning people

- They get non-medical advice from their doctors
- They take financial advice from friends
- They take care planning advice from non-professionals
- They rely on Google
- They get medical advice from the wrong doctors

Recommendation: Now that you have your "Advisory Board" use them to think through what advice you need and where you are getting it from. Re-evaluate what advice you need and check certifications and philosophy. Do not be afraid to make changes. This is about you, or your loved one's needs.

The devil is in the details. Your plans for aging in place might start with your definition of where "Home" is and your definition of "aging well." It may be in the details of a longer-term medical prognosis you will need to deal with. Get a real education and honest professional assessment around issues of understanding the medical diagnoses and your long-term care prognoses of the real costs of care.

Your housing options: Is it time to consider "Assisted Living" as a potential new "home"? Be honest about how our Aging Journey depends on others at a significant level of detail. This is what we have previously referred to as "Burden of Care," and it has become an important issue in healthcare. We assume others will successfully play supporting roles in our journey of aging, but they may not be aware of the operational realities of playing these roles. It just may be logistically impossible for them to do so.

Recommendation: Write everything down. Your assumptions, your decisions and rationale behind these important decisions you are making and the conclusions you are reaching. Review them with people who have the real expertise you need and those who may need to make decisions on your behalf.

Understand the importance and power of Managing Risk. Today the big focus in our healthcare system, and major emphasis in the home care industry, is around keeping you out of acute care, whether it's an admission or readmission. This is where the buzz is, and much of this book is devoted to the subject.

People focus on the events (planned and unplanned) on the journey of aging rather than the whole process. Manage the things that put your journey at risk on a day-to-day basis. People and our systems for care focus on the situations not the outcomes we need to manage to keep the situations from happening.

For example, an unfortunate but very common example is when a senior falls and breaks his or her hip. With a broken hip the hospital deals with the pain and a hip replacement. The Rehab gets them back on their feet. The Home Health/ Agency (PT, OT, Nursing) helps them complete their recovery. None of these interventions impacted the things that put the senior at risk and resulted in the broken hip in the first place.

Recommendation: Have a comprehensive assessment completed that assesses your total risk for potential speed bumps, potholes and sinkholes on your journey. But make sure there is a plan in place to address each and all of these areas.

CHAPTER FOUR

Scoring for Success: When Science Combusts with Art

Almost two decades of research and thousands of individual cases have come together to create our methodology for defining and managing care needs. The Senior Helpers LIFE Profile™ is helping to change the way we think about wellness and engagement in the world. In the last chapter I described it in concept. That is what is important – it constitutes a comprehensive assessment of risk and how you use that assessment to figure out what care is needed, who can provide it and how it should be delivered and documented.

Making Sense of the New World Order: Discharge & Recovery Science & Art Changing the Face of Home Care

Living in New England we are spoiled by a world class medical environment. One night we hear on the network news about the new "Medical Home," where Boston's Dr. David Levine is betting on better care for patients by discharging directly from the ER to home. Levine maintains patients get the same treatment and quality of medicine through technology and house calls, while at the same time undergoing faster recovery by being in familiar surroundings. This can all be delivered at more than 50% less cost to our healthcare system. Is this the future of care across the country? How soon might it become a universal reality?

A few days later the *Boston Globe* announces three business titans are joining forces to remake and redefine the delivery of medicine. How can we not take notice when billionaires such as Jeff Bezos, Warren Buffett and Jamie Dimon are turning to world famous Dr. Atul Gawande to help us better understand our role in experiencing healthcare. This was a huge story, although at the time it lacked specifics.

I appreciate these stories because they speak to how rapidly the face of care is changing, especially when centered in the home, and it requires us (all of us) to take active responsibility for our care. In Greater Boston, we see Home Care going through a significant evolution. Recovery at home has moved from concept to reality, as the process of discharge from hospitals and rehab directly to home earlier in the recovery is being rapidly adopted.

Yes, costs are reduced, but seniors now go home faster. This new trend is impacting the landscape of rehabilitation and changing the concept of what it takes to recover and continue to age safely at home.

How Far the "Warm Hand-Off" Has Come

In the language of my industry, the "warm hand-off" has meant the process, conversations, protocols and engagements of care around discharge from hospitals or rehab to home. What is the game plan for recovery and who are the players? In the past, the objective of the hospital was to manage the immediate medical need. The rehab was there to drive recovery and home health (the visiting nurses and therapists that come to the home) to support the tail end of recovery with physical and occupational therapy, with home visits paid by insurance.

This continuum of care has now been disrupted and we are all in the process of figuring it all out; seniors, families, and industry professionals. The role of the hospital has not changed significantly, although days spent in the hospital have dropped precipitously across the board.

At the rehab, the focus has shifted from "full" recovery to support until recovery can safely continue at home with home-based therapy from Home Health. Again, the pressure is to get you out quickly, all while achieving the same outcomes. This fundamental change in where you recover places new burdens on the institutions that are discharging. They have to get it right because the penalties for readmission are becoming rigorous. Going home delights patients: most love the thought of recovering at home. But what about the "warm hand-off"? What does it look like? Who explains it and who manages it for the senior? The fact is, private Home Care has emerged as the most impactful "go-to" resource for recovering at home.

We are in a showdown around how our current system of care is struggling with integrating Home Care into the continuum *and* having it make sense for both seniors and professionals who are referring home to their patients and clients. This is because at least in the short term, Home Care will remain outside the Medicare/Medicaid/insurance system; the senior will be footing the bill. Home Care agencies are not yet integrated into the "protocols" of clinical care or the medical record technology. The "warm hand-off" process is manual and takes time and effort. The definition of a Home Care Agency is all over the place. In Massachusetts, there are no standards for how an agency functions, delivers it services, manages its services or trains its staff. This last point is absolutely critical because when seniors are footing the bill, and professionals are referring to a Home Care Agency, how can you be sure you are working with a reliable and credible partner in care?

I often feel I'm on a well-worn soap box when I write about the lack of standards and licensing for Home Care. But the fact is, credentials, certification of Aides, Aide training, recruitment philosophy, care specialization, nurse case management, client-centric service backed by 100% guarantee, insured and fully employed caregivers and much more, are not just nice-to-have standards of doing business in a Home Care Agency. *They are the absolute must-haves.* These are the table stakes. You need to be an informed consumer when choosing Home Care. Be inquiring, inquisitive, bold and brassy. Do whatever it takes to manage this part of your recovery and aging in place.

Aging in Place: Making Scores Work in Your Favor

Every day part of my job is to help my clients and their families make important decisions about their care plans at home. As a son (along with my siblings), I also am instrumental in helping my parents successfully age in their home in Virginia, nearly 500 miles from where I live. Both of these come with huge responsibilities and accountability.

My end game has always been to be an outspoken advocate for successful Aging in Place. This is not just a nice concept, but also the objective of my company. Programs such as "Going Home Safe" were conceived around the premise of mitigating risks and preventing readmissions (and admissions) to acute care. It also engages families and the extended care continuum in keeping seniors safe and secure during the critical 90 days after hospitalization.

I have witnessed firsthand the wisdom and power of managing risks at home. Yes, it can be formidable for seniors and families to dissect these risks and get them under control. Yes, it can be incredibly time-consuming to master nutrition programs, medication management, safety and scores of essential issues critical to the big picture of being safe while recovering at home. But we *do* understand and see the endgame in getting it right. The "homework" of analyzing and resolving the risk factors right under our loved one's nose is worth every hour spent determining them.

When it comes to the bigger picture of aging in place, and seniors managing risks at home, there are significant new insights impacting success and failure.

"Thriving" is Taking on a Whole New Meaning

Houston-based, Performance Based Healthcare Solutions™ (PBHS™) research into the cycle of readmissions over the last 20 years. Two decades and 30,000 plus case examples have resulted in a detailed understanding of risk attributes and thresholds in five distinct "categories. This scorecard identifies the risks a person must resolve to create a platform for success. The individual category scores are important. The goal of reducing risk to a defined threshold is the linchpin.

The Scorecards are All About Removing Risk

The premise of the methodology is simple. It is all about assessing and removing or mitigating risk. At its core it is analyzing the factors that stand in the way of a senior being safe and secure, medically managed, having personal care needs met properly, being emotionally engaged and independent at home. In analyzing and putting a score to those factors, a properly-conceived plan of support and care can then be defined put in place to reduce and eliminate the risk. The fact that all of these risks have been identified, quantified, and made "score-able" is the breakthrough.

My parents have been role models for aging in place; they have mastered the art of it. I feel lucky to be in a position to help them do so with more than words and encouragement, but also with concrete support that I can deliver to them that is both data driven and clear.

In the last few years we have baked in a philosophy around risk which began with the launch of our "Going Home Safe" program. That journey has been further shaped and sharpened with the science of managing risk through the PBHS™ methodology – the LIFE Profile™ - to impact all of our care. Here is the point: Outside support such as Home Care on its onw or within the context of a broader circle of care can be a well-crafted "surgical" response to risk rather than a broad generic support.

Home Care has the potential – more importantly – the obligation to combine the science of care with the best in care techniques and care management. It is this combination that will redefine the possibilities for seniors at home. It will give them more information and command than ever before in order to make informed decisions over their destinies to age in place safely, securely and gracefully. Let the data show the what, let the care show the way. Let's dig into the data!

Safety Risks at Home. What's Your Score? Applying the New Science in Home Care.

According to the Administration on Aging, in 2017 more than 20% of men and 48% of women over 65 lived alone. This should not be surprising given the fact that during the majority of our adult lives we are taught to live independently. Why uproot yourself from familiar places and spaces just because you're a senior? The fact is living alone comes with some inherent risks, which are often reported in polls like in "The 10 Dangers of Living Alone."

Some of the issues in this list are understandable; we are social creatures and living alone may cause isolation that can lead to depression and anxiety. With empathic intervention some of these may be fixable. Other factors on this list can be easily remedied. Seniors living alone are at greater risk for falls, accidental overdose of medication, and higher rates of malnutrition. Some may be unable to maintain basic housekeeping, either because they are physically unable or mentally unmotivated to do so.

When I hear about these particular issues it simply reinforces why I do what I do. There is no reason why any senior, alone or not, should be in danger of risks that can be both easily identifiable and readily removed.

My clients are often stunned when I tell them there are more than 144 potential safety issues that can sabotage their well-being at home. There are materials and minutiae to get managed every day around three core areas: what physical condition they are in, the task(s) they are performing and how their environment helps or curtails them. Obviously, this picture is different for each senior.

When we begin to evaluate seniors in relationship to their homes, we can now get very granular about the risks that confront them at every turn. When they enter and exit, are steps too tall or awkward? Are doors secure and all railings and ramps in place? And surfaces conducive to every weather condition? There are at least seven things that can happen just going in and out of the house.

Fire prevention in the home can be easily overlooked if one is not actually evaluating it. Are the smoke detectors functioning? Where are the fire exits? The kitchen is often its own war zone when a stove, oven or microwave is well used but poorly located. Flooring is important, often area rugs are culprits. Inspecting for unsafe items, especially if randomly placed, can pose critical risks that are easily mitigated. What are the risks that a bath and simple toilet pose? We are able to dissect a score of issues from poorly placed doors, the need for an elevated toilet seat, strategically placed non-skid tape, and better devices that can prevent a host of injuries in that one space alone.

By now you are getting the picture. These are intersections of form, function, risk and removal. It is the result of years of study and evaluation, insights and collaboration. There is no reason why seniors cannot be totally safe these days thanks to this kind of rigid analysis.

Working with the safety scores, a program of support and care can potentially reduce the risks in play. We can quantify safety "outcomes" so informed decisions about care are no longer made in a vacuum but against real requirements that yield real results. This provides a tremendous checklist to ensure capabilities and capacities are in sync. When good sense is being reinforced by great science it is good for all of us and makes home a real possibility for a "game plan for life".

Technology will Save the Day (Not Just Today But Also Tomorrow)

There have been seismic shifts in Home Care. Amazon purchased upstart PillPack for $1 billion. Best Buy purchased GreatCall for $800 million. These acquisitions brought both retailers full swing into the "older adult market." Best Buy acquired a series of apps and services and access into MedCoach, CheckIn Calls, Urgent Care, Wellness Calls and others. All these companies have gained access to millions of customers, while at the same time banking on seniors with needs for "support," which are only going to accelerate in the future.

One of the great things about being in senior care is being in the parallel universe of new technology like those just purchased by these huge conglomerates. With sites like "Aging in Place Technology Watch" and links to Silicon Valley startups, the Home Care industry is an incubator for technologies being developed to address both real and perceived needs of seniors. Professionally, I am drawn to those that focus on Aging in Place - two in particular: solutions that enable seniors to live longer and healthier lives at home, and innovations that address the risks that prevent them from doing so successfully.

There is no dearth of ideas and well-intentioned entrepreneurs when it comes to providing alerts and monitoring devices for seniors. Many are under development and the market is filled with options, including significant attempts from Amazon and

Google. But have they solved it with Alexa devices, reminders, notifications and drop-in calls? There had been an in-home robot whose dual mission was socialization and reminders. After spending $73 million, it collapsed.

Are any of these solutions enough? Or even the right answer? Can an expensive alert system prevent a fall, or will it just report there has been one and notify the right people? Will a robot predict a situation before it becomes a problem? Will a signal that Mom has successfully opened the refrigerator every six hours also show there is spoiled food in it? More importantly, that she did not eat any? Will a monitor in every room reveal that a loved one hasn't paid the heating or cable bills? Or that the laundry piled up for weeks in a hamper?

This is by no means an attempt to disparage technology because there is great technology that is already available and visionary work is now in the pipeline. It is to say we must be smart about how we leverage it and understand how it supplements hands-on care. Rather than seeking a technological panacea, perhaps we should be applying science and human logic.

13 Things and a Score that Matters

In evaluating Independence and Autonomy, there are 13 tasks to calibrate for risk. They include what most of us consider mundane, but they are activities that add up to a safe, satisfying, secure and self-reliant life at home for a senior. They embrace the basic ADL's (activities of daily living), like dressing, toileting and bathing, and simple acts of mobility around the house, such as using the phone and paying bills. They include shopping for groceries and meal preparation, getting the laundry done, the house cleaned, and taking the garbage out.

Most importantly, the score includes being able to manage medications and other conditions, including getting to doctor appointments and other necessary places. We know that if an individual scores above a certain base, there will be a high probability for successful independent living.

Here is the tricky thing about any of these activities – there is embedded risk that must be managed: Getting the trash out of the house and to the curb could mean a fall. Making a bed in a tight area can result in a painful or awkward turn, leading to a sprain and demobilization. If Mom or Dad cannot manage the use of the phone, who will they call for help? If the bills are not being paid to Comcast, the cable and connection to the outside world is shut down, meaning that "cutting edge technology" will no longer be connected. Every single activity and task of independence and autonomy has a unique consequence for a senior.

The great news about the science and being able to profile and score these activities is this: we can now clearly calculate where additional support and help is needed. In uncovering where the potential risks are in these routine daily activities, the well-informed conversation about managing the risks can constructively begin.

Said differently, we can be surgical in our structure of care instead of broad and general. This should translate to better care plans focused on the right care at the right time done in the right way. It's important to be aware of the next technological gizmo or widget to come on the market. But that doesn't mean we should not incorporate them into the mix, but only if and when it makes sense to do so, such as when it reduces risks.

When the Burden of Caregiving Becomes a Risky Proposition

We hear it every time we get on an airplane, "In the event of a loss of cabin pressure, an oxygen mask will be automatically released. Be sure to secure your own mask before helping others." Why? Because it makes perfect sense to be in a good place ourselves before we take on the burden of caring for someone else, even if that person is right next to us.

Our clients are like family. This makes our job both enormously rewarding and incredibly daunting. The "daunting" part is from the personal relationship we have to a family caregiver; a spouse, an adult daughter, or an extended family member who has agreed to take on critical caregiving responsibilities on a part-time or full-time basis. Listening to their first-hand experiences, we learn to adjust the many roles they expect us to fulfill and we have been able to learn a lot.

In an incredibly emotional process, the more data and science we can bring to bear the better equipped we are for the diverse roles as chief comforter, field guide, and care expert. With science, expertise, and a significant network of resources, we can surround clients and their families with a circle of support to help them successfully assume the incredible role they have as caregiver.

Anyone who has been a family caregiver knows all too well it can be an emotional roller coaster. On the one hand it is a clear demonstration of love and bold commitment and can be a very rewarding personal experience. On the other hand, research has shown it to be enormously stressful, where the demand of continuous care results in exhaustion and constant worry, with caregivers more prone to weight gain, chronic illness, and high blood pressure.

Assuming a caregiver role for parents while simultaneously juggling work and raising children can lead to an increased risk for depression, as well as an overall decline in the quality of life and financial stress. Citing sleep deprivation and postponing their own medical appointments, it is not uncommon to hear my clients remark, "My husband has Parkinson's but now I'm the one in the hospital!"

Family Caregivers: Endangered Species

The Caregiver Action Organization reports statistics on family caregivers, including what makes up this population and where the trends are going. Here is a snapshot today:

- The typical family caregiver is a 49-year-old woman caring for her widowed 69-year-old mother who does

not live with her
- 20 hours per week is the average number of hours spent caregiving
- 23% of family caregivers report health issues
- 72% report not going to a doctor as often
- 40% to 70% have significant symptoms of depression
- 6 in 10 family caregivers are employed, yet 1 in 5 report having to take a leave of absence

One might take away from these statistics that caregiving can be hazardous to your health, and it can be. It is only in the last few years that our profession has actually given a definition to all of these statistics. It is called Burden of Care (BOC).

According to Randy Bartosh, Co-Founder of Houston-based, PBH Solutions, "Burden of Care is the physical, psychological, financial and emotional stressors associated with the caregiving experience. Today, it is the single most neglected aspect of healthcare in the over 50,000 patients we studied, and its results can be devastating for the quality of life, health and success of the family and the care receiver."

Stated another way, if the family caregiver is *not* prepared and supported for this enormous task and all the inherent burdens that come with it, both the caregiver *and* the senior, are at risk.

When Science Intersects with Common Sense

We have previously covered the potential risks seniors face when recovering at home. Success is challenged by risks we've defined by broad categories of safety, medication management, and activities of autonomy and independence.

Now We Can Layer in a Critical Piece That Includes the Assessment for Burden of Care

There is a five-sentence clinical overview of Burden of Care that drives home the reality of it from a medical perspective. I could confuse you with terms about hypothalamic-pituitary-adrenal (HPA) axis and the adrenergic sympathetic nervous system (ASNS), or the release of glucocorticoids from adrenal cortex and the profound effects of stress on our cells and organs. But the bigger point to be made about the Burden of Care and risk is that it is critical to understand when, how, and why family caregivers need additional support in their important work and why there needs to be a focused plan in place to help them.

When considering Burden of Care, there are 16 potential points where a senior may be at risk. Some of these issues seem like no-brainers and seem to only require some common sense and ingenuity to solve them. Others are more complicated and require training, education and skilled intervention.

Here are some important questions we need to ask: How can we simplify or reduce the routines around the senior to lighten the demands on the caregiver? Can we become more systematic or save time in our approach to visits, meals and other tasks? Are there ways to increase the "time away" from care duties, giving caregivers respite and space to breathe and refresh themselves? Are there extended family members who can be called upon to augment care in a concerted fashion? Are there ways to optimize durable equipment, assistive technologies and other innovations to reduce where possible the physical stresses and strains of caregiving?

Other caregiver interventions may involve strategies outside the immediate family. Are there community support systems and resources worth exploring and ways to plan and maximize outings and trips?

There is a full spectrum and category for formal and informal counseling, caregiver validation, wellness coaching and disease education. These curriculums are designed to empower caregivers, provide them a platform to discuss situations of importance, and give them the valuable tools they need for succeeding in their intensely personal journeys of care. Each of these 16 intervention modalities represents a focused level of support and delivers proven techniques that help mitigate caregiver isolation and promote emotional equilibrium and comfort.

There is no one-size-fits-all approach to Burden of Care because no two family dynamics are the same. The risks to a family caregiver and a senior in the home are intensely personal and the solutions are customized. Once risk is assessed and all available resources are applied in a specific manner, we can then discuss the remaining needs – the risks left unmanaged. This gives the family caregiver a clear picture of what is reasonable to expect of themselves and where to enlist outside support.

There is so much to consider when deciding to become a family caregiver. As one of the most important journeys you will ever make lies before you, be buoyed, heartened, comforted and confident from this exciting and proven combustion of science and common sense.

Ask Yourself Again How Big, Bold & Boundless Do You Want Your World to Be?

While Quality of Life can mean a hundred different things to a senior, we must be able to reveal, explore, discuss and ultimately score important individual needs – which are different for each individual. For some seniors, quality of life can be an expression of who one is, how one looks, exercises and generally feels. This can be in combination with a spiritual well-being and connections to a broader community. A meaningful day might include activities that promote relaxation or making time to improve specific skills. It can be something specific, like successfully completing a 1,000-piece jigsaw puzzle, or revisiting old joys by joining a mahjong group. The goal is to identify the "calendar for life engagement" and follow-through on 40-50 activities that connect a senior to active living. The beauty of this process is that it works across those aging in place, those suffering cognitive decline, and through each of life's transitions and stages of aging. Quality of

Life ultimately depends upon a senior's ability to "engage in life" regardless of how this is specifically defined.

Let's take "Don" as an example. Don has been a widower for about a year, and still lives by himself in the family home. During a wide ranging quality of conversation we are able to discern a lot about Don and his interests. We learn that making time for Don to connect with friends, watch football, work in the garage, spend time on his boat, grab coffee and the paper with buddies, visit a war museum, donate time at the library, get a meal of smoked sausage, and more are all things that are important to him. We determine activities that he enjoys and needs for a positive and successful journey of aging. Certain activities in his week will let his endorphins rip and put a smile on his face.

What Don requires are specific challenges that put him in control of his journey of aging. When these are presented to him on a calendar, what appears is a robust quality of life of his own making.

This is not "Betty's" calendar, because Betty just moved into an assisted living community. Betty's calendar is reflective of ongoing monitoring of her Parkinson's disease, along with visits from old friends and walks with budding acquaintances. It will include resident gardening projects, a weekly computer class so she can Facebook her grandchildren, popcorn and movie nights, afternoon naps, and co-chairing the Ladies' Society at church. Betty's days will have a natural flow designed to mitigate the anxiety of being in new surroundings while complementing her natural friendliness and ease in meeting new people. What Betty sees in her calendar is maintaining a quality of life of her making that is secure, relaxed, flexible, and in her control. The Quality of Life (QOL) Analysis completes the picture of what life can be like for a senior who chooses to age in place and how to make it a successful journey.

When Don combines all of his scores, including Quality of Life, he will be equipped to experience a lot of "good days" and many more and better days. Living alone, it is important he take his medications and keep up with doctor appointments. His Home Care plan already zeroed in on these specific issues. Now it will also include the activities that are valuable to his journey, such as a trip to the Park, or fishing off the local pier and making that smoked sausage dinner for friends.

For Betty, now in an assisted living community, her plan will reflect supporting the successful long-term integration into her new environment. This includes continuing to maintain nutrition, medication, exercise routines and monitoring of Parkinson's, in combination with her plan for active engagement in the assisted living's activity program and other personal valued activities such as supporting her to maintain her chair duties with the Ladies' Society at her church.

Quiet quality times pieced together like a puzzle make each day fully lived. Nuanced layering from the Quality of Life explorations make them uniquely agile in helping Don and Betty live boundlessly.

Chapter Checklist for Success

When you think of ways to help manage risk at home through a structured plan of care and support, consider and be honest about:

- What safety risks do you worry about at home? Be specific about these, especially if you live alone or live with a spouse or loved one who may not be fully capable of supporting your safety risks.
- What concerns do you have about medication and general medical management?
- How would you honestly assess your independence and autonomy as you read this chapter?
- How would you honestly assess the burden of care you place on those around you because of your current physical or medical requirements?
- How would you honestly assess your engagement in life?

Back to your PLAN:

- How have you prepared for important conversations?
- Who will be involved?
- What outside resources are available to you down the road for support?
- What is the expanded circle of family support you can

count on?

- What role will each of you play and how will decisions be made? How will you determine what next steps to take?

If "Home" is Not the Best Option, What are the Current Considerations?

Continue to define (and refine!) who should be in your "Circle-Of-Care," because now you know the risks and concerns that need to be managed. You need to know who in your circle is best equipped to help you, including friends, family, professionals, medical/clinical support, neighbors and resources. Consider their roles and why you include them.

CHAPTER FIVE

Home Care: What Really Matters and Why

Today, Home Care is becoming a desired option for recovery from a hospital stay and, more importantly, for aging in place. Even if a current or future diagnosis is complex or uncertain, the power of "Home" is compelling. Why is this? Because at the heart of great Home Care are exceptional caregivers. Exceptional skills training enhance innate gifts to make caregivers the game-changing factor for seniors aging in place at home. They are also being complemented by emerging technologies that make seniors safer and more empowered.

A Fresh Lens: Study Puts Considerable Value on Home Care

Because I work in the business of Home Care every day, once in a while I need to be reminded what a young industry this is. Owning and managing two uber-busy offices in motion 24/7/365, serving clients in 75 communities and recruiting, training and certifying top notch caregivers for complex cases and complicated schedules, I am the first to lose sight of how Home Care is evolving in significant ways.

"The Value of Home Care" is a comprehensive study released in collaboration with the Global Coalition on Aging and the

Home Care Association. If you work and care for seniors, are a senior yourself, or an adult child concerned for the welfare of an aging parent or loved one, this study should give you pause. It did me, and I'm in the business. While there are formidable statistics and lots of data to pour through, there are several perspectives worth sharing.

Home Care is still "Young" and Emerging

While long-established in Massachusetts, it is often easy to lose track of the time and the players while working intensely within this industry. Terminology flutters and evolves, confusing both professionals and consumers; especially around differences between Home Health Agencies and Home Care Agencies. A Home Health Agency refers to a skilled medical service usually consisting of Physical Therapy, Occupational Therapy, Nursing, and Speech Therapy. In most cases it is a covered (insurance) benefit but can also be privately paid. When covered by insurance, Medicare or Medicaid, Home Health is doctor-prescribed.

A Home Care Agency, on the other hand, provides support for Activities of Daily Living (ADLs) such as bathing, grooming, continence care, medication assistance, etc. (Think of this as activities which require the caregiver touching the individual being cared for.) It might also support Instrumental Activities of Daily Living (IADLs), like meal preparation, light housekeeping, errands and transportation.

Home Care services are usually paid for out of pocket by the individual receiving care, or through a Long-Term Care Insurance policy. In other words, private-pay. The landscape can get very confusing because some Home Health Agencies call themselves XYZ Home Care (and some of them also offer private pay Home Care services). I am an agency that fully employs and insures my caregivers and staff. Other Home Care business models could be referral agencies or registries. It is important to understand the distinctions, because the differences can be profound.

Lack of Licensing in Home Care Requires Vigilant Consumerism

Agencies cannot be compared based on price because if they are there may be added costs and liabilities incurred which fall outside the quoted hourly rates (employment taxes, unemployment contributions, workers' compensation, etc.). Most importantly, THERE IS NO LICENSING OF HOME CARE AGENCIES in Massachusetts and critical factors like training, caregiver competencies and oversight can vary significantly, as can service offerings and quality guarantees. It is why I am always a proponent of "looking under the hood" and being a smart consumer when referring to or negotiating the services of a Home Care company. Being a young industry, however, has distinct advantages. We are always in innovation mode. We are bold and entrepreneurial, forward thinking in the use of technology, and ahead of trends affecting seniors.

Regardless of the state you live in, you should be doing full due diligence on your provider – even if your state is regulated.

Providing Choices Means Flexibility & Nimbleness

The great thing about Home Care is its flexibility, its ability to zig and zag at a moment's notice, all while presenting a menu of options that fill a home-full of needs. We also live in an uber-economy, where consumers and professionals are accustomed to outsourcing almost everything. We have to be flexible in our approach to care as well as cognizant that a growing number of families are "getting things done" in a variety of different ways. Caregivers need to provide to their clients a broad range of hands-on care, a growing list of little and big "stuff" in and around the home, and an assortment of activities that are as eclectic as our clients and our caregivers. In return, caregivers learn how to play gin rummy and mahjong and maybe a thing or two about cod recipes native to Jamaica. Caregivers prepare, plan, and play, cleanup, organize, and take-out, clip, cue and clean-up, dress and discuss, make, maintain and monitor, write, read, remind and reminisce, ship and supervise, clean-up, arrange, assist, answer and escort. The list goes on and on. Caregivers provide simple meals and manage and monitor chronic conditions, including complex diagnoses of Alzheimer's, dementia and Parkinson's. This is clearly where Home Care excels and belongs in the circle of support for seniors.

Home Care Fulfills the Desire to Stay at Home

Over 80% of Americans in their early 70's own their own home. When asked, 90% of seniors stated they wanted to stay in them, to age in the familiarity of communities they know, as it comforts them. *The Boston Globe's* Robert Weisman often pens front page stories about today's seniors and his "Not So 'Senior' Moments" is a robust portrayal of today's local Senior Centers and Councils on Aging. These centers of life for seniors are absolutely hopping these days; dropping bingo nights for boxing and swapping the sedentary for Zumba. Right now our elders are aging in a completely different way than their parents did, and being able to stay at home and get to these places of community, continuity, and camaraderie is made possible with help from Home Care.

Home Care Fills Gaps of Care with Vibrant Solutions

In the past, families traditionally took care of elders. Today, it is a struggle. There are fewer family members to provide it, families are living much further apart, and there is simply a tsunami of seniors in need. Home Care is emerging as a vibrant solution to this in a way that is strengthening preventative care and reducing doctor visits by 25%. Home Care never intends to come between seniors and their trusted specialists, but companies like ours have become skilled and use science to assess risks at home. When individual care plans have case manager and supervising nurse oversight, issues can be anticipated before they materialize. When family members are partners-in-care, the support team becomes more invincible.

Caregivers Become Potent Antidotes to Loneliness

The great thing about being an independent company is being able to forge services that fully respond to the evolving needs of clients, while deploying the amazing skills of individual caregivers. Tracey Crouch was Britain's first "Minister for Sport, Civil Society and Loneliness." Her articles in *The Guardian* cited the extraordinary challenge of looking at loneliness from a country perspective. She portrays loneliness as "an indiscriminate disease that has become an epidemic." Closer to home, the acclaimed neuroscientist, John Cacioppo delivered a compelling TEDx Talk on the "Lethality of Loneliness." He simply argued that as a species we are not built to be alone, and are meant to connect and be joined together. The former Surgeon General, Vivek Murthy on CBS *This Morning* cited how loneliness in seniors can morbidly affect dementia, depression, anxiety and cardiovascular disease. Stimulation and engagement through Home Care is a potent prescription for this epidemic. A caregiver is more than just a provider of personal care; they are also a point of critically needed human connection – of touch, conversation and interaction.

We Alleviate and Unburden

Today, more than 44 million Americans serve as family caregivers for someone age 50 and over, spending on average more than 24 hours a week providing care. The impact of these responsibilities is profound. Seventy-percent of caregivers cite depression.

The beauty of Home Care is in its flexibility. It is not all or nothing. Resist the urge to do 24/7 math. First, the goal is to establish the needed support, then look at the full system of care to see what can be managed by resources in place and where Home Care can fill in and alleviate the burden. Home Care *must* be totally complementary to and part of the system of care. And it can because it is tailored. To be successful it must meet the needs of the family, and to be valuable it must engage the senior and, where appropriate, the extended family or loved ones in the plan. Remember the zig and zag! Plus, a stunning career may lie just around the corner.

The fact that the Home Care industry now represents a fast growing career opportunity for woman and men is an absolute bonus in my mind. This study anticipates that by the year 2024 there will be a 24% growth in caregiver jobs, the most of any other sector in the U.S. It will be a vibrant workforce representing all walks of life.

Caregivers I have worked with have come to the field from different countries, sensibilities and backgrounds, but similar hearts. They have endeared themselves into new family orbits, and claimed caregiving as second or even third career. I realize

I might be a bit biased about this study, but it seems to me that whatever new insights it sheds on Home Care, we shine.

Training the Angels: Finding Those to Do the Amazing

In my opinion caregiving is one of the hardest jobs in the world. I know this because it's my job to find, recruit, develop, train and empower a broad team of talent to be caregivers for a diverse group of clients. Sadly, right now we have a scary shortage of caregivers (data shows a range of 25-40% labor shortage). It is even more worrisome when experts from the Department of Labor and Bureau of Statistics suggest that between now and 2024 the demand for Home Care workers will need to add more jobs than any other single occupation. Where, I ask, do we look to find these angels?

WorkingNation, a national group that uses multimedia to address work and employment changes, partnered up with PHI, a research and consulting non-profit, and its #60CaregiverIssues.org initiative, to launch a multi-year campaign to raise awareness for the shortage of Home Care workers. It calls attention to the importance of caregiving as a career, and makes the case for advanced training and improved wages.

Backed by significant data, this is a bold and ambitious undertaking for both organizations. It has stunning promise for hundreds of thousands of caregivers. It has the potential for impacting the nature of work, the image of the care, and the lives of the care providers, their clients and families. It will surely cast caregiving in a whole new light.

If the campaign fulfills its objective, caregiving will be fittingly honored and given its due. It will be appreciated as one of the most difficult and respected positions one can discharge. It will be front-burnered as a potential career for college students seeking training, benefits, mentoring, fast- tracking and immediate feedback. More importantly, it will call attention to the urgent crisis we have, right now, for well trained, certified, and empowered caregivers.

Robert Espinoza, VP of Policy for PHI, originally reported his observations in the *Huffington Post* in an article titled, "8 Signs the Shortage in Paid Caregivers is Getting Worse." This set the stage for his campaign strategy, which was declared in another article, "How Training and Multimedia Can Fix the Home Care Shortage". Espinoza and his WorkingNation partner, founded by venture capitalist Art Bilger, are heavily invested in this national campaign. They want to change minds, hearts, attitudes and, ultimately, the future of long-term care. Their media blitzkrieg will be about a lot of things: facts, trends, quality jobs, pay, employment respectability and the undisputed need for advanced training for Home Care workers. This compelling campaign will resonate because it will convey the power of caregiving, by telling the story of one caregiver at a time. As part of this effort, Livia Gershon of WorkingNation reported in her article, "Reimagining Masculine Work in a Post-Industrial Future," how caregiving for seniors in their homes is totally legitimizing the role of men in the emerging role of the "emotional labor force." No longer is caregiving being seen in strictly the feminine domain. We need to embrace this concept because we need these men in the workforce.

The campaign is adventurous, imperative, and intrepid. A YouTube video thrusts caregiving in a whole new light, presenting Home Care as a game-changing opportunity for women looking to make a difference. The video, "Do Something Awesome," is a fresh, smart, and real insight into how Home Care is a valuable and valued employment option. What Working Nation, 60CareGiverIssues.org, and PHI are doing is important work, and we all have a huge stake in the success of this campaign. No Home Care company can afford to be a bystander in all of this.

With a considerable footprint in the New England region it is our responsibility to constantly look for the best and brightest. We need talent fresh out of nursing school, and seasoned veterans with particular skills in areas like complex care, Alzheimer's and dementia, Parkinson's and end-of-life. We need to be out in front with our own community workforce development programs for training future CNA and HHA talent; because the need is now.

Because we have such a clear understanding of seniors and aging, we grasp not only the crisis in caregiving, but our role in mitigating it. Caregivers are essential to our ability to deliver innovative services and unparalleled care, so we are absolutely rigorous in our hiring practices. We have a multi-step selection process, and comprehensive seven step e-verify protocol background check and on-boarding process; because the angels are embarking on serious work.

The philosophy of care should begin with an approach to caregiving; meaningful work means caregiver readiness. This translates into intensive training and orientation for every caregiver we bring on board. This includes full days of tests, exercises, evaluations and skill development around topics ranging from fall risks, blood-born pathogens, meals, nutrition, ADL evaluation, medication and administration, to legal policies and procedures, elder abuse and more.

As Home Care becomes more valuable and valued for the journey of aging, certification and extraordinary competency in supporting complex diagnoses will become requisite. Caregivers with superior skills and advanced understanding in Alzheimer's, Parkinson's, ALS, dementia, will be mandatory, expected, and absolute game-changers. Every September is Caregiver Appreciation Month, and honor is due to all who give their time, talent and treasure to caregiving our seniors. This is just another reminder that we need to be vigilant in our recruitment, training and empowerment of our angels.

When The Caregiver Shortage Hits Home

In his book, *Who Will Care for Us?* M.I.T. economist and human resources expert Paul Osterman examines trends in the labor force market for caregivers. He basically concludes, "It's an absolute train wreck waiting to happen." As owner of a Home Care Agency I believe it's a train wreck that is here now.

While a recent *Reuters* article affirms many of Osterman's assumptions, I have experience from two perspectives. I know how difficult it is to recruit and retain qualified caregivers for work in private duty Home Care, and I have seen how consumers have changed the dynamics and demands of that care. These changes have been recent, significant, and, in my opinion, irreversible.

Caregiving in the home is unique for several reasons. Unlike caregiving in an assisted living, skilled nursing facility or hospital setting, it is challenging to contract a caregiver for set hours, firm schedules and guaranteed pay, week in and week out. In my industry, caregivers usually work for several agencies at the same time in order to cobble together a work week that makes sense for them financially. This is hardly what one would call a secure work environment.

Additionally, caregivers often pivot where and for whom to work based on salary. I am constantly watching wage and pay scales in my market and am keenly tuned to incentivizing my caregivers based on their experience, commitment, flexibility, and other hard and soft skills they bring to my organization. What Osterman points out in his book, as have others in the industry, is that caregivers now understand they are in short supply. This fact is changing the negotiation dynamic, which also has implications on the workplace culture.

Private duty care is also a fickle environment that depends as much upon personal chemistry as it does caregiver skills and expertise. A squabble or disagreement with an extended family member can result in a dismissal of an exceptional caregiver. In a larger, structured environment, that same caregiver would simply be transferred to another patient or floor. This may be totally arbitrary and unfair, but it is the reality of the job.

As my industry has responsibilities to both clients *and* caregivers, we have had to recalibrate our business in significant ways. We now recruit caregivers for specific hours they can rely upon for work, and we guarantee them the opportunity to grow in the job and earn more. We do this because unlike caregivers in any other setting, we are also asking more of them.

Caregivers in private duty Home Care are unique because they are asked every day to make important and independent judgment calls when they are on the job. Unlike a mega-supervised setting, like a hospital, our caregivers fly solo in our client's home. They must be prepared and confident to make on-the-spot decisions involving scores of little and big issues. Our clients depend on them to make the right ones, as do my supervising nurses and case managers. This is also why we look for mature, seasoned and "life-experienced" caregivers, and demand that each be Home Health Aid or Certified Nursing Assistant trained.

A major shift, as noted in the *Reuters* article, has been in the sheer acceleration of demand for care in the home. These decisions are more frequently being made in crisis mode, when a major medical event has happened and a family is in chaos. As an agency we must have a rapid response to staffing these emergencies with uber-caregivers while we are also developing the critical, customized care plans. This requires that we create a stable of caregivers ready to deploy for these events, which we call "startups". This has disrupted our former business model and presented a new set of challenges. We now are hiring caregivers as staff and there will be emerging expectations from both clients and caregivers.

At the heart of private duty Home Care is the client, whose demands and expectations are also changing in this environment. For us, the two client issues that will always drive us are great care and safety. As caregivers flex their agendas we will not always be able to staff unconventional shifts. We will have to honestly decline some of these cases. Our caregivers have kids, car pools, schools, and outside responsibilities themselves. They, too, are juggling, scrambling and scheduling. We respect their busy lives and must balance that along with the wishes of our clients.

We pride ourselves on matching up caregivers with seniors and the wishes of extended families. Great match-ups require more than sending a skilled CNA or HHA to perform a job – but an understanding of human nature, experience in the business, and the quality of being an excellent listener. This does not take place overnight. In this new Home Care environment, transparency, honesty, and flexibility are required from everyone in the mix.

As new dynamics take shape in my industry, forces around it are helping to change attitudes. PHI International, WorkingNation and 60CareGiverIssues.org are collaborating in a multi-media, multi media effort to thrust caregiving in a whole new light, while presenting home care as a game-changing opportunity for women, and men looking to make a difference. We need them to be the best they can be because they are doing incredibly important work. Because of these variables, we anticipated the change in market dynamics and we prepared for them. Our readiness in staffing reflects where clients are coming from and the shifting landscape of caregivers. Our philosophy of care and intensive caregiver training speak to our continuing commitment to safe aging in place at home. The caregiver shortage might be hitting home, but by each of us understanding what is at stake, we have a better chance that great care will always find our homes.

When it Comes to Home Care: The Beauty of Keeping it Simple

One of my jobs is to keep on top of trends in our industry that can influence care to our clients. I am a voracious reader and student, staying constantly on top of technologies being introduced in our field and methodologies in caregiving. While I am eager to take it all in, I am also conscious of keeping it all simple. I have learned that while delivering world class Home Care is serious business, it does not have to be complicated.

Because keeping home care simple for families to understand, access, and benefit from is ultimately what matters.

No time is it more important to take a deep breath and keep it simple than over the holidays, which we often refer to as "OMG" times. This is the returning home of adult children and "sandwichers" to find parents and family elders not aging well in place. For months they have been perched hundreds or even thousands of miles away. What they hear during Sunday calls or in energetic emails is "Everything is fine," "Can't wait to see you," when in fact it is far from what they see when they walk through the front door. Then, it's "OMG, what has happened to Mom and Dad!!" Survive "OMG" by keeping it simple.

The Simple Art of Listening

I like to call this "listening between the lines" because sometimes seniors say one thing, but in reality are saying something else. By asking simple questions and listening with true intention, it is amazing what can be gleaned from simple conversations.

As you move through the holidays and relax into familiar roles around the house, asking about neighbors, foods you know your mom loves, or restaurants, weekly games and outings you know dad enjoys, you are discovering the patterns of their daily lives. Do they get out of the house with frequency? Are they engaged in the community they love? Do they see long standing friends?

I guarantee you will begin to see a pattern of daily life that will or will not include good nutrition and healthy diet, and a contentment for where they are in their journey of aging that engages the outside world–or maybe not. If you are concerned about the "not," then perhaps it is time prepare a plan of support for your loved one at home.

Keeping the Plan Simple

When it comes to setting up a plan of support for a parent (who is at best skeptical), I tell clients that a simple plan is usually the smartest plan. As I am quick to reassure clients, one of the best things about aging in place at home is that families decide who comes in and out of it.

We encourage our clients to keep their support plans simple by focusing on a few important components: the plan to fulfill their current needs, and the type of caregiver who will be the best fit for their loved one. Sure, we can speculate about future needs, but first let's focus on the right now. If a loved one has trouble with one or more basic "Activities of Daily Life," or ADL's, putting a plan together to address these is not complicated. They might include help with walking or otherwise getting around the home or outside. The technical term for this is "ambulating." It can also include:

- Feeding, as in being able to get food from a plate into one's mouth.
- Dressing and grooming, as in selecting clothes, putting

them on, and adequately managing one's personal appearance.

- Toileting, which means getting to and from the toilet, using it appropriately, and cleaning oneself.
- Bathing, which means washing one's face and body in the bath or shower.
- Transferring, which means being able to move from one body position to another. This includes being able to move from a bed to a chair, or into a wheelchair. This can also include the ability to stand up from a bed or chair in order to grasp a walker or other assistive device.

Another category of tasks, called Instrumental Activities of Daily Living, or IADL's, can also be easily guided or completely supported at home. These might include:

- Managing finances, such as paying bills and managing financial assets.
- Managing transportation, either via driving or by organizing other means of transport.
- Shopping and meal preparation. This covers everything required to get a meal on the table. It also covers shopping for clothing and other items required for daily life.
- Housecleaning and home maintenance. This means cleaning kitchens after eating, keeping one's living space reasonably clean and tidy, and keeping up with home maintenance.
- Managing communication, such as the telephone and

mail.

- Managing medications, which covers obtaining medications and taking them as directed.
- Putting together support to address one or more of these issues is what we do in Home Care, and most companies provide significant flexibility in providing and changing hours of care.

Simple is Sometimes Easier than You Think

Mileha Soneji, a product engineer from Pakistan, gave a riveting and personal TED Talk a while ago. In it, she shared how she designed a simple human-centered solution for her uncle with Parkinson's. She observed his struggles with walking on flat land, yet his ease and mobility in negotiating staircases because of the continuous motion it required. Her solution was to design a 3-D illusion staircase on flat surfaces so he could walk unaided by a walker. She was not trying to "cure" Parkinson's, but simply to make her uncle's life easier. It was a noteworthy message.

If your loved one has been recently diagnosed with Parkinson's, your "OMG" visit may be more complex than you imagined. A holiday visit may seem overwhelming, but sifting through what is important and right in front of you is sometimes easier than you think. Today, there is so much more that is known about Parkinson's care than ever before, and many caregivers are specially trained and equipped with tools, education and insights that speak to the specific demands of this disease. Nutrition planning and eating well at appropriate intervals are essential. Maintaining medication and exercise routines are absolutely mandatory.

We have seen how specific exercises can build power, strength, flexibility and speed in seniors with Parkinson's, as well as lessen symptoms of this disease. It is why companies like ours have local relationships with fitness centers that offer inventive programs, education and classes like Rock Steady Boxing that strengthen and tone seniors with Parkinson's. And thanks to technology, Home Care companies can now surround and engage families to whatever extent they want to become an active member of the caregiving team. Families can be 10 minutes away or 10,000 miles away and be engaged in the care of a loved one.

The Beauty of Simple Results

In recent years, Dr. Eric Coleman, Professor of Medicine at the University of Colorado, has become one of the most influential voices in healthcare self-management. He has developed a particularly sophisticated program of coaching when it comes to recognizing the influence of family caregivers. Adopting aspects of his approach has impacted how Home Care companies like ours train, educate and support adult children and extended family members actively engaged in caring for seniors. This is where the concept of "simple results" comes in. Deploying the basic philosophy of Coleman's Care Transitions Program (CTP), families are supported in structuring realistic goals for helping loved ones successfully age in place at home. What does Mom or Dad really want to do? Get back to normal activities after surgery? Re-engage with friends at the Senior Center on a regular basis? Eat more nourishing meals to gain strength for gardening outdoors? Return to walking in the dog park? Customized care plans support these goals. Nurse-supervised caregivers serve as de facto team leaders. Adult children and "sandwichers on the scene" are armed with confidence, skills and training. This team is too formidable *not* to be successful!

The Beauty of Simple Connections: When High Tech Meets High Touch

In 2018, a team of high-powered Boston tech entrepreneurs, having suffered frustrating and even tragic personal experiences trying to monitor and support their own parents from a distance, announced the development of LifePod, a "virtual assistant to caregivers and a virtual companion to seniors." Powered by Amazon's Alexa Voice Technology, the "Pod" would enable a three-way relationship to do routine reminders and check-ins as well as perform some fairly sophisticated tasks; like arrange transportation via Uber, remind seniors of medical appointments, provide family with daily check-ins, play games, read audiobooks and the news, play music, and more.

LifePod planned to improve fall detection, not only detecting it, but starting a conversation with the senior, asking if he or she was OK. If not OK, a preconfigured chain of events follows, alerting the senior's caregiver and, if needed, initiating a 911 call. If a senior says something like, "Oh, I'm not feeling well," LifePod will probe and try to help. If LifePod gets out of Beta testing, finds a level of funding (crowd and free market) and gains traction in the busy tech space, perhaps it will have a place in the Home Care industry. It is unlikely, however, that it will ever replace the demand for high-touch when it comes to caregiving and companionship. Requiring no technology or Wi-Fi, the powerful connections caregivers make with seniors is outside of staggering, and no technology, regardless of its superb capabilities, will supplant the simplicity of the human touch.

If you fear your upcoming family get-together might come with "OMG" moments, perhaps it is wise to just keep in mind that keeping it simple sometimes is the best solution.

The Parallel Powers of Compassion, Communication, and 40 Seconds.

Compassionomics is more than just an interesting book; it is a fact-based proposition that makes a powerful case for how 40 seconds can change the dynamics of care in our healthcare system. As an owner of a Home Care Agency, I see stunning parallels to my world view.

Dr. Stephen Trzeciak is an "intensivist" and in his own claim meets people "at the worst times in their lives," when they require extreme life-saving intervention just to stay alive. He is also a scientific researcher who provided, in a profoundly personal way, incontrovertible proof that the medical profession is in a "crisis of compassion." Among the statistics cited: 50% of Americans believe healthcare providers lack compassion, two-thirds of people experience our healthcare system without compassion. Disturbing as it sounds, compassion is less than 1% of all communications between physicians and patients.

Dr. Trzeciak and Dr. Anthony Mazzarelli co-authored *Compassionomics: The Revolutionary Scientific Evidence that Caring Makes a Difference*, which provides a compelling case for the effects of compassion on patients, the cost of care, and the well-being of providers. It is an important read for all of us who subscribe to patient-centered care, the importance of self-care management, and the powerful intersections of art and science when it comes to "care" in every sense of the word.

This new thinking engaged exhaustive research. Drs. Trzeciak and Mazzarelli use science and qualitative and quantitative data to do more than just suggest that compassionate care can buffer stress related disease, lower the severity of pain, enhance immune response, and get people to take better care of themselves. Science has already shown that when there is Patient Centered Care, the overall cost of care goes down, there are fewer hospitalizations, referrals to specialists and requests for diagnostic tests. I totally get the power of compassion to influence the economics of care.

What about the "art"? The art of compassion is in what Trzeciak and Mazzarelli refer to as the "40 seconds." This is because they submit that 40 seconds is about all it takes to make a difference in changing the communication between patient and physician, and ultimately the outcome of care.

Today, the crisis of compassion is due to, so they suggest, physician burnout. This is defined as an inability to make a personal connection; a condition Trzeciak realized himself. Thanks to evolved medical records, so much time is spent staring at computers that many doctors have simply forgotten how to make compassionate connections and to "communicate care."

In the TEDx Talk, Trzeciak talks to the magic of "40 seconds," and gives a moving example of it in a script read in a patient/physician meeting about cancer treatment. It is stunning to hear how this simple yet effective script, coupled with 40 seconds of communication, can transform a critical visit.

I write often about the science of great Home Care because we know we have years of research and a solid foundation of studies to inform us about what works and why. In truth "the science of care" is the easier aspect of my business because of the extraordinary engine of our LIFE Profile™ Methodology. We can dissect, discern and mitigate hundreds of risks for seniors in most any conceivable home or living situation because we have reams of scientific evidence to back up our human analysis. But this "science" is not what is important to you. How we apply our science to the personal situation for your Mom, Dad or loved one is all that matters. Do we have the caregiver who is sensitive to your lifestyle and can support needs at the ready? Have we really been listening to your concerns? Have we heard you? Here is where Home Care is at the critical intersections of compassion, art, and science! Trzeciak defines compassion as an authentic desire to help. This is an emotion that is in constant parallel with empathic communications in the development and delivery of personalized care plans for our seniors. The holistic support and experience for our clients trumps the transactional needs of the day. Of course, medication management, bathing, grooming and meals are absolutely essential; but so are emotional connections and being able to successfully answer the question "Was this a great day for you?"

One of the most optimistic theories Trzeciak and Mazzarelli put forth in their data-driven pursuit to infuse health care is this: compassionate behaviors can be learned. They challenge everyone in the arena of care to test the theory of giving 40 seconds of compassion and witness the difference in the giver and receiver of these communications.

This is provocative art, rooted in compelling science. Every day the caregivers at Senior Helpers make compassionate connections with our seniors and families. It is reaffirming and heartening to know that our work is on a parallel plane with these powerful new theories in "Compassionomics" and care management. It should give seniors and families great confidence that there are providers that "get it," where so much success depends on unparalleled communication.

Technology Must Be a Friend of Home Care, Not the Enemy

Laurie Orlov is a tech industry veteran, elder care advocate and founder of Aging in Place Technology Watch. *Market Overview* is a 10-year review she released in 2019 which studied the impact and influence of technology in the senior living sector. The report is wide ranging and robust, and a must read for anyone in the field who is curious, concerned, or simply wondering how, where and when technology will play a role in the journey of aging.

I have watched the startup tech sector closely; particularly those companies whose stated mission was to "disrupt" Home Care. I admit skepticism about why the VC and investment communities could be attracted to home care, despite the allure in knowing that 9 out of 10 of seniors choose to age in place at home. Because I'm in the business, I know how difficult it really is. It is not for the faint of heart, and often contains a tangled web of challenging and unpredictable moving parts. It is intensely personal and requires a tremendous and proactive care management process for it to work.

Autopilot Approaches Will Fail

I was not surprised by Orlov's summation of the decade in which "over-heated investment – culminated in an unprecedented $200 million of failed, bungled, or pivoted Home Care startups – leaving the traditional Home Care industry largely unchanged."

In the last 10 years several Home Care rock-stars jumped full-throttle and with significant fanfare into home care, such as "Honor" and "Home Hero" out of California, and "Home Team" in New York, to name a few. Two have dramatically shifted their business models, and Home Hero shuttered with $23 million still in the bank. In venture vernacular it was disruption meeting reality.

The common denominator of all these adventures was a failure to recognize the personal nature and hands-on management required. At its core, Home Care is a people business with respect to clients and employees: flexibility, respect, training and personal touch are all that matter. It is about people not process.

Home Care is not about serving seniors through "customer acquisition" but from developing trusted relationships with elders and professionals, such as discharge planners at skilled nursing facilities, resident care directors at assisted living communities, and elder law attorneys who are intimately aware of what seniors and their families are facing. Developing loyal and long-term clients comes from being a reliable, trusted, accessible resource for families in crisis, and a familiar and reputable face in the community and in the continuum of care.

Most importantly, Home Care is about caring; this involves the critical engagement between our senior and the caregiver.

This is not an algorithm. This is not about a 1099 "worker" and a fragile senior connecting because of a scheduling convenience. Caregivers forge deep bonds with the families in their care, and this is not by accident or mathematical formula.

The many ways people contribute to this magic recipe are what make Home Care challenging and hard to do well. Yes, some will subscribe to the "uberization" of the industry; but when you get up close, it is people caring for people.

Success for a caregiver in Home Care is more than just a full weekly schedule. Caregivers tell us that it is about respect and training for them as professionals. They want their experience and expertise to advance particularly in areas of Alzheimer's and dementia care, Parkinson's Disease and complex care. This is important to them as this is a career, not just a job.

The other piece about Home Care that these "disruptors" eventually realized is this: Home Care is a difficult business to scale. At its heart it is local and good companies that are firmly rooted in the communities they serve. Agencies like ours develop strong ties with community and providers - the Senior Centers, Council on Aging's, VNAs, Assisted Living communities, short-term Skilled Rehabilitation and Nursing Centers, and other supportive services for elders. Every town is different and it takes time. Let's face it, real technology disruption is coming. It just may look different than people think.

People want to age in place. That being said, let us pressure technology to influence four colliding issues. These must be reconciled in order for seniors to do this successfully: Regardless of wealth, the economics of care are daunting for a family. How can technology make us smarter about how we orchestrate it? Many elders will ultimately require a large "volume of care" – but this does not mean that a hands on, one-on-one support is the only available solution. What role will technology play in designing our strategic approach? "Intelligent" Technology– monitoring devices, platforms, applications, wearables, software—will insinuate itself into care strategies. We must be laser-focused when we embrace it.

Regardless of shifting family structures and geographies, the demand for information about care, in real time, is becoming non-negotiable. How will technology help meet these new requirements?

This translates to three critical boxes Home Care must check to be successful for you or your loved ones. Understanding risk profiles and managing these issues requires us to excel at understanding individual risk profiles, because Home Care is intensely personal. When we understand risk, we can craft smart, focused, strategic solutions for people that balance the right care with the right method of care. In doing so, we are ultimately balancing the cost of care and the burden of care.

Skilled eyes to interpret: technology is never enough by itself. We need skilled eyes to interpret, reconcile and act. Local case management of care and support, with a hands-on touch, will always be important – regardless of whether you are 50 feet away or 1,000 miles away.

Well-Trained Caregivers – There Can Be No Shortcuts!

We know, and Orlov's report confirms it, there will always be technology evolving in the pipeline of senior living; technology that connects us, enhances our quality of life, increases our autonomy and independence, eases the burden of care, and hopefully reminds us of what is important in our lives. We will continue this conversation for sure. The way I see it, Home Care does not need technology to "disrupt," but to augment, support, and help us be the best we can be.

Home Care as an industry has deep and broad variations. Regardless of the style and type you engage, it should make care easier to manage, instill confidence in making a situation better, and should connect you to the set of resources needed to achieve the agreed-upon outcomes.

CHAPTER SIX

Seven Journeys

Each Journey of Aging is unique and distinctive. Each tells a different story of urgency, resilience, independence, family engagement and decision-making, contingency planning, could haves and would haves. These seven journeys represent seven special seniors whose lives have influenced and affected our lives as much as we hope our caregivers and care have affected theirs.

Special Seniors and Their Journeys of Aging. Why They Amaze, Enlighten and Inform.

We have focused on the rich lives of the following seniors to illustrate how diverse today's older population is, and how differently each elder approaches their Journey of Aging. Because of them our health and Home Care industry must be incredibly good listeners; coming to each elder's story with open ears, eyes, and hearts. We know there is no one great answer to aging well and successfully, and we cannot even be adequate in our support if we are not open to all options we are prepared to offer. Read about these lives and consider what decisions you might make if you were in a similar place. What does each of these seniors have in common? What are the keys to the success in each "story"? What or where was there a critical "tipping point" that made a significant difference in the outcome for each elder? And keep in mind these things:

- Understand how each senior is supported by a unique "Circle-of-Care."
- How everyone in the "circle" has an important and defined role to play.
- Crises will arise; and contingency plans should always be in the background.
- It is important to have back up; this is different from contingency planning because everyone needs a "sub" in the Circle-of-Care. "More" care doesn't always translate to better care. A strategic and focused plan for care and support is more essential than simply throwing more money (more care) at a situation

Meet Mrs. G: "Active Aging"

I often brought Mrs. G a Shabbat Challah from a well-known kosher bakery, or flowers, on her birthday. There was simply a special connection I had with her, and I felt that although I was not directly her caregiver, that in some respects I *was* taking care of my grandmother. After all, I knew all about her children and where her grandchildren went to school. And she was always frank with me: "Your beard is terrible, stop growing it."

We had a special connection and I always enjoyed being with her. She was a fiercely independent woman who lived in an independent living community. She needed only limited care, maybe 90 minutes a day to help with morning routines. This support was ongoing for several years and was intensely personal.

While this was a small case for my Agency, the consistency of staffing was all important to its success. It was pronounced in this relationship because it ensured the scope of care was totally successful given the small window of time in which we engaged to deliver it. The bond between the caregiver and Mrs. G was intense. It was essential the caregiver be able to spot when things were not quite right the minute of walking onto the scene.

The case took a turn one day when Mrs. G, now 94, was "not quite herself." A trip to the hospital was immediately determined through a call between our on-site caregiver in concert with our nurse supervisor overseeing the case. The hospital visit turned into a stay in rehab and then further recovery at home with initial 24-hour care support. This care was cut back to a 12-hour shift then ping-ponged back up to 24 hour support because of a fall Mrs. G. took one night. Clearly, her needs were shifting and required new evaluation.

Mrs. G's community had an assisted living option on its grounds and it was now time to have a family conversation about the role it might play in her future journey of aging. Being fiercely independent she was reluctant to move into another unit and building; fearing she would lose vital connections with her "independent living friends." At her age, would this "transition" present more of a downside than upside in her ability to age in place successfully? How would this all play out with the least disruption to her treasured routines? What would be the impact financially and in terms of care options down the road?

What Made the Difference and Why

It turned out that timely conversations with her Circle-of-Care, intelligent decision-making, and taking advantage of the alternative options ultimately served the fiercely independent journey of Mrs. G. In this particular case, in the assisted living program of care, she could change living units but would not require 24/7, 12-hour support or any private support. Care would be "on demand" or "at large." Simply put, she would be using it as she needed it and calling the shots herself.

Assisted living proved to be a win-win. It is more autonomous than private care and Mrs. G had control over all of it. She's doing great. She still enjoys her old friends yet can now actively participate and engage in a broader array of programs and events held on the grounds. She has all of her needs met while joyfully aging in place on her own terms. While we are no longer part of her "Circle-of-Care," we do stop in and check on her now and then. And of course, there's always the Challah to deliver.

Meet Mrs. Z: "Complex and Complicated Care"

Mrs. Z had been a prominent academic who sustained a spinal cord injury in a critical and life-threatening accident. After rehab and recovery she was sent home under the care of an agency inexperienced in what was fully required to support her needs. After recover, she had gone home with an agency who failed to understand the magnitude of his needs and requirements for specific routines in care. Soon, skin breakdown problems caused subsequent hospitalizations and skin grafts. During these procedures our agency was consulted and contracted for Mrs. Z's care.

Arriving at her home, we discovered it had been completely retrofitted: equipped like a hospital room with a comprehensive set of capabilities including a bed with ceiling mount Hoyer lift that extended to a fully and appropriately appointed bathroom. We immediately set to work to develop and define a comprehensive Care Profile that would become our roadmap for care. We would follow it religiously, and as it adapted over time, so did our care. The routine we initially established included a personal 24-hour specific regimen of care, exercises, nutrition and medical follow-up. Our caregivers, over a period of three days, were specially trained on all the issues facing Mrs. Z. Within days they were "case ready" for Mrs. Z to get back to the work and be safely rehabilitated to her maximum physical limits.

Eight years later, Mrs. Z is doing well at home. She continues writing, publishing, speaking and advising even while working hard to maintain her physical capacities through rigorous caregiving, aggressive therapy, and a constantly evolving plan of care involving nutrition, exercise, engagement in life, medication management and more.

Mrs. Z continued to work until her retirement. Our caregivers were a support team that coaxed, coached, and enabled full autonomy so Mrs. Z could orchestrate her needs to a greater extent as the days and months went by. In the many years we've supported Mrs. Z, there have been no gaps in care. Sure, caregiver transitions have occurred. The case is demanding and rigorous; some caregivers are a good fit, others not so much. One original caregiver remains on the case. Staffing is challenging because along with the work of the caregiver, it's also the results of the "team" that count. Target staffing is five aides although four could cover. The goal of a fifth aide is to be available in the event of vacation or other time off needs.

What Made the Difference and Why

Communication, teamwork and a constantly refreshed approach to care have been the most critical attributes of Mrs. Z's care. Extensive and specialized training separated those that could meet the rigorous demands and schedule that defined Mrs. Z's case. She sought aggressive rehabilitation after her surgeries and was eager to see results to set her on the path to recovery. She knew her limitations but wanted to get back in the game. When you have a client setting a high bar, the pressure is on us succeeding, and, you want everyone on the team working towards the same goals.

Creating a team culture among the caregivers enable us to discuss Mrs. Z's evolving needs and schedules. This alignment has proven invaluable in discussions about what skills are required as Mrs. Z experiences her ups and downs, or where is the need for conditioning in specific parts of her motor activities. The team bonds around sourcing new staff for the case, supporting therapy techniques and weaving in and out of Mrs. Z's day-to-day life. All of this gives heightened meaning to quality of care and an extremely high level of autonomy and independence to Mrs.Z The care is under her direction, allowing her to be in control and independent.

Maximized communication between caregivers and the Agency, the Agency and Mrs. Z, as well as between Mrs. Z and the caregivers, ensures that the overall system of care with extended family works. It is not a cobbled together system, but an integrated circle of care because Mrs.Z is fiercely determined. We put the best players on her team to rival her grit because beyond being caregivers, we're also her loudest cheering squad.

Meet James: "A Love Story as Old as the Ages"

The back story here is as timeless as any ever told. When the love of your life is gone, often it is hard to find the will to live; the energy to get up in the morning, or to simply carry on.

When you are of a generation where sexual orientation has not been fully embraced, and much of your adult life may have been spent in lonely or "together" isolation, losing that love of your love is even more devastating. Such was the case with James and his husband. James had been living at home with his husband for decades. They loved to travel, dine out at the newest and chicest eateries, binge-watch the Sunday morning political shows, and don "Go Pats" attire for the big games. Although they had been married for years, they had come to accept minimal family ties and involvements.

Now into their 90's, their declining health prevented them from doing the activities they treasured. They sought out the support of a Geriatric Care Manager, who could help frame and guide their future health and well-being. James began to show signs of dementia and required more help around the home, and his husband experienced frequent trips to the ER for "this and that." Both were absolutely committed to aging in place, but they would need support in order to do so independently.

The Geriatric Care Manager (GCM)[1] recommended Home Care. Home Care initially "checked off all the boxes for support." It began with minimal support during the day for shopping, meal preparation and transportation, to ensure James got to and from important doctor's appointments. Sadly, although James was the weaker of the two, his husband ended up passing away due to a series of unforeseen and critical hospitalizations. James was devastated, and it quickly became apparent that not only had he lost the love of his life, but he had lost his love for life and the will to live. Working hand in glove with the GCM, Senior Helpers strategized a new level of support for James that took into account his failing emotional state and the consequences it played on his physical well-being. Our care became 24/7 and our support followed James wherever he happened to be, especially as his health declined and he ended up in the hospital – rehab syndrome.

Finally, and with full agreement with everyone caring for James, a last episode of declining health sent him to rehab and he did not come back. Full care didn't seem to make sense and private care was no longer necessary as palliative care was now involved in a skilled nursing community.

What Made the Difference and Why

In this case, the involvement, engagement, care and coordination with an experienced GCM made the strategy for Home Care more powerful. This was a complicated situation in which two men had been living fiercely independent lives for decades. They were determined to age in place and have as much control over their destinies for as long as possible. A creative GCM who knows the way around the healthcare system, combined with a strategic and agile plan for responsive Home Care, made keeping James' agenda possible for as long as it was practical. Having a team approach to care can only make care stronger.

The fact was, the caregivers became so attached to James, this incredibly kind and fun-loving soul, that even after their services stopped, they continued to visit him in the Skilled Nursing community on their own time. James was so grateful for the companionships that he left his caregivers his treasured state-of-the-art Big Screen TV, which now hangs proudly in our office. Go Pats!

[1] Also referred to as Aging Life Care Professionals

Meet Mrs. P: "A Powerful and Dignified Journey"

For many years Mrs. P was an active and engaged resident in a well-known and highly-regarded assistant living community. That was until her struggles with ongoing falls began. The community attempted to set up safety precautions for her to help reduce those risks, but for one reason or another the falls continued, and her overall health deteriorated sharply.

After multiple trips to the hospital and rehab, the family found themselves in need of supplemental care, post discharge. Initially 24/7 care was established for Mrs. P, until it was reduced after two weeks to 12-hour daytime care. As an Agency, we had advised differently because Mrs. P was still at high risk for a fall should she attempt getting up at night for a trip to the bathroom. The family, however, decided differently. Within 24 hours, Mrs. P was unfortunately back in the hospital due to an overnight fall. If Mrs. P was to age in place, as she desired, the best place for her was going to be a return to her assisted living facility under 24/7 care.

After these falls, and in light of her deteriorating overall health, Mrs. P. was also placed on hospice. With 24/7 coverage her scope of care fully supported all aspects of her Activities of Daily Living (ADL), such as bathing, grooming, and teeth, as well as many Instrumental Activities of Daily Living (IADL), such as paying bills, keeping her apartment clean and organized, and providing good companionship. This support was coordinated with the experienced eyes of a team of caregivers and within the context of the assisted living community. This is where communication among the "Circle-of-Care" kicked into high gear. A nurse-driven and supervised care plan drove the overarching strategy of care and support for Mrs. P. Case management staff of Senior Helpers was in constant communications with the family, the care management staff of the assisted living community and the hospice agency. Documents and documentation specific to Mrs. P. were created to meet the needs of the varied providers and our Agency took the lead for sorting through and parsing the appropriate details and requirements.

What Made the Difference and Why

Clarity, coordination, communications, conversation, and understanding the important role everyone had in Mrs. P's life were critical to her particular journey of aging. Mrs. P's personalized care plan was tight-knit, involving our Home Care Agency, a highly regarded hospice provider, and a caring staff from her assisted living community. Experience has demonstrated that with the combination of Home Care and hospice care, life can be filled with intention as seniors feel more alive and more human than their illness or condition has allowed them to be over the months or even years. Mrs. P. certainly had her share of painful falls and unplanned trips to acute care, but she was now "home," exactly where she wanted to be.

With a select group of caregivers specifically trained in end-of-life care, and working collaboratively with a hospice provider and an assisted living community long familiar with Mrs. P, together we were able to deliver profoundly personal care. We always encourage families to share this time with each other and to leave the caregiving and medication reminders and the details and stress related to those tasks, to us.

Communication among all caring for Mrs. P. had to be pitch-perfect. Aides from one shift to another had to know exactly what was going on, documentation logs had to be crisp, clear, and on point, and service providers, doctors, hospice and family had to be kept in the loop with the right information in real time. This would allow and encourage them to be simply families and loved ones, while sharing memories and stories.

The Hospice Medical Director noted, "You do what you say you do. I go in, I ask questions and your aide knows the answers. And, if the question pertains to a different shift, they can go to your documentation logs and find the answer. I do not see this often."

This level of clarity of what was important to other providers, to the family, to the client and to the assisted living facility, enabled communication to be focused on delivering the right information to the right people. Caregivers understood the scope of care, the mix of providers and what the objectives were for Mrs. P All were kept front and center to support her successful aging and passing in her home at the community.

Mrs. P remained engaged in community life to the maximum extent possible for the rest of her life. Her caregivers served as support for engagement; not in lieu of it. This made it possible for her to do what she could, when she could, how she could, and without pressure, all with respect for her journey of life and her love for participation in it. For the most important journey of all, Mrs. P. was cared for with dignity and deep respect.

Meet Mrs. R: "Sometimes a Journey Requires a Team"

What do you do when you want to relocate your 98-year-old mom, Mrs. R, across the country so she can age closer to all of her living family?

If you are smart, as a first step you hire an expert Aging Live Care Professional (formerly called Geriatric Care Managers) to orchestrate all of the details required to manage this complex situation. These include the massive details of transition and establishing relationships with required providers to ensure all the bases are covered for every conceivable emergency. These professionals are exceptional, working with families to ensure those often elusive "goals" for aging in place are discussed and achieved. For aging in place today, it is equivalent to dotting the i's and crossing the t's.

When Mrs. R arrived in Boston, she was truly frail and required full assistance. Though wheelchair bound, she was, however, by no means shy or retiring. She had had round-the-clock care and support for several years, and was familiar with what was involved with this kind of support. With a two-person assist, she could readily and easily communicate her needs and wants.

Our Agency was one of three the GCM asked to pitch their services to the family. Having met with both Mrs. R. and the family, and gaining critical professional insights from the GCM, we decided to take a different approach to support for mom. Rather than merely proposing two caregivers performing 24/7 care, we instead highlighted a solution that targeted five areas: 1.) Minimal caregiver transitions, familiarity with each caregiver as a Priority Team Approach, 2.) Roles and responsibilities defined across the team of case management (Home Care and GCM) and aides to ensure all were working towards the same goal, 3.) Case Management to ensure a well-managed plan providing maximum flexibility and nimbleness, 4.) Communication that is central to every aspect of care delivery, and 5.) Economic Cost Management, because although finances were not a priority for the client, fiscal responsibility was important to us.

The GCM managed key relationships for Mrs. R, including those with her Concierge PCP (primary care physician) for the coordination of appointments, follow-up visits, supplies, prescriptions, medication management, communications, and other issues. In coordination with that relationship, regular Home Care Nurse Case Management visits were provided by our Agency. Additionally, we directed the shopping for food, meal preparation, nutrition, and other items. Respect for this "system of care" was paramount. Communication was direct with the family but required ongoing and real-time discussions to keep all informed. Care logs were reviewed weekly, and all parties kept current. Caregiver transitions were managed proactively to balance team dynamics with quality of care. Tradeoffs were managed in both directions in order to maximize bonds and relationships between Mrs. R and her individual caregivers. It became quickly apparent that caregivers are life-givers and life-long bonds and rich attachments were being formed; Mom was the center of all this attention and care.

After three and a half years, hospice became involved and roles shifted. Hospice became the lead and the Home Care Agency continued to provide care, comfort and support services. Mom rallied and was discharged from hospice. Ultimately, Mom passed under the care of the Home Care Agency.

What Made the Difference and Why

Nurse-Led Home Care Case Management, great caregivers, GCM Leadership, Team Respect, Communication, were keys to this exciting journey of aging for Mrs. R. But care ultimately made the difference. At all levels it is ultimately a deeply personal bond between the caregivers, the family, the Agency and the client. People will always trump process and protocol. Care must always be nimble and ready to adapt and adjust at a moment's notice. It must be poised for success and ready for surprise. In this case, systematic communication about care, people, process and objectives kept a large diverse set of participants aligned on mom's needs and family priorities. In reflecting with the family after Mom passed, they were pleased about her final years, and their ability to share them so fully with her. There were 22 people at the funeral, including five from our Agency. You see, Mom had become our family too.

Meet Mr. G: "Aging Wherever 'Home' Is"

A well-known assisted living community called us about a resident who was displaying signs of slipping into an advanced stage of dementia. Mr G is in his 70's, and his wife and daughter were active in his care and were hoping to continue his stay in the community. They were eager for him to maintain his activities and engagements while there. The community, however, was concerned about his potential for "wandering", and his increasing needs for cueing and redirection, especially when he was confused and thus exhibiting behaviors that made others uncomfortable.

While Mr. G suffered short-term memory loss, and required mild assistance with ADL's, like dressing and bathing, his hearing, speech and swallowing were all considered good; and he was personally engaging. Our care started with some minimal overnight stays and some of Mr. G's issues abated. We considered our work done.

Mr. G then made physical contact with another resident and we were called back in for a 72-hour one-on-one observation. This support continued on an ongoing basis, with nights being problematic. Mr. G had established a cycle in which he would wander into other rooms and become confrontational. This behavior is not acceptable in community settings, and a more intensive approach to support was obviously required.

We initiated a team approach to Mr. G's support. Working closely with the assisted living community and the concerned family members, we began providing 24/7 support. We met weekly to establish an open line of communication; discussing trends and activities that seemed to trigger behaviors in Mr. G and creative ways we could abate or avoid them.

Working as a team, it was critical that community staff be familiar, as our trained caregivers were, with issues like "sundowning"; when people with dementia are unable to distinguish day time hours from night time hours. Understanding the behavioral consequences of dementia would be an important part of our combined caregiving strategy, as we all had to be on the same page.

During the day, our caregivers would accompany Mr. G to all three meals, providing much-needed companionship and grounding. Mr. G had his own "activity cart" and throughout the day caregivers would keep him entertained and engaged with the items on it, while at the same time also helping him exercise. Overnight, caregivers would re-direct Mr. G. if he tried to wander into another resident's room, gently encouraging him to get more sleep whenever possible.

What Made the Difference and Why

A nurse led and directed care plan, team work, and client-specific trained caregivers were a huge part of our success in making Mr. G's aging in place possible for two and a half years. Senior Helpers worked with the staff at the residential community to develop a plan to enable Mr. G to age successfully in place for as long as possible. It was a focused plan and it was agile; built to change as needed for any number of reasons.

Having caregivers specifically trained in dementia was absolutely essential to Mr. G's Care Plan. Managing challenging behaviors, and recognizing that behind those behaviors there could be a myriad of issues (from sleep deprivation and medication issues, to dehydration and hearing loss) are all part of caregiver training for dementia.

Understanding and managing the art of "direct and redirect" can save situations like those in this assisted living community and at home. All of this specialized training benefited both Mr. G. and the other residents of the community.

With a well-managed care plan we eventually reduced services and concentrated care during those time periods when Mr. G's behaviors would most likely come to the surface. While being "care- responsive," we were also financially responsive. After many months we reduced our care to 12-hour overnights; then nine-hour overnights. Medication changes eventually allowed Mr. G to sleep through the night without wandering. Mr. G is now in a skilled nursing facility. His dementia has worsened and his condition now demands clinical care. We believe we had a hand in keeping him "at home" for as long as possible through a positive approach to care that engaged a true circle of professionals.

Meet Mrs. F: "Aging with FIRE"

Mrs. F was truly annoyed. She was placed into a fine assisted living community by a loving family and every minute she was there she was steaming mad. She didn't want to be there and made it obvious to everyone around her, including her adoring family members and the caring community professionals trying their best to engage her in life and activities at the residence. After a stay in acute care, and recovering in physical therapy on an out-patient basis, everything in her 93-year-old body was screaming a phrase we have heard many times in our industry,

"I do not want to go back there, I want to go home!" So this was our job and, challenge; to get Mrs. F back home.

Mrs.F was determined to prove to her family she could successfully live on her own. But how do we get her back home safely, and make sure she can stay there safely? We took our assignment one step at a time by initially assessing all of the risks her home presented to her, especially given her age, as well as recent medical issues and current condition. What did her initial transition look like? She lived in a two-level home, which meant there were stairs involved. She wanted to drive again. What were the implications there? She was on an oxygen tank. How was she going to drive a car and manage an oxygen tank? A caregiver needed to physically assist her up and down two steps just to enter and exit her home. She had to learn how to both navigate steps and manage the oxygen tank in the car. She also had to agree to carry back-up oxygen. just in case. The details looked overwhelming, but her determination was strong.

If Mrs. F was willing to conquer the risks we had identified, then we could build her a "Going Home Safe" plan that acknowledged her extraordinary passion for getting home and staying there. Much would depend on her openness to work with a customized Plan of Care that acknowledged the risks her home imposed, and her willingness to adopt that Plan of Care to successfully work around them. This Plan of Care also would go a long way to convincing her family that she could live on her own.

The original shifts for caregiving that we set up almost two years ago are exactly the same as those in place today. And the reason for this is because they work. They are successful on every level that counts and on levels we did not count on. We provide Home Care for Mrs. F from 11 am – 5 pm "on most days." Since coming home from rehab, Mrs. F has been wildly successful living on her own. Today, she no longer requires oxygen. We first took Mrs. F. to the YWCA twice a week for exercise. She didn't stay for a full session, but to her credit she did what she could. Today, she stays for a full work-out and goes gangbusters.

These days she is "out and about" every day in her community; running errands, visiting the Council on Aging, going to meetings, classes, functions and church every Saturday. She makes dates for shopping ventures and trips. She's on the phone daily with friends and family, and never misses a birthday or chance to send a card or letter. More importantly, she's managing her own bills, medications, and doctor's appointments. She gets her own breakfast in the morning and our caregivers clean up when we arrive on the scene, before prepping for lunch and dinner. She tells her caregivers where she needs to be and when.

What Made the Difference and Why

The right Plan of Care, assessment of risk, caregiver compatibility, and passion for independence are what has made a difference in Mrs. F's journey of aging. If one of these ingredients was lacking, the Plan would not have worked. Home Care has suited Mrs. F extremely well. This is a relationship of great mutual respect, admiration, and love. So much so that if her three caregivers are not available for her, she will simply cancel services for the day. There was an intense respect for Mrs. F's need to be independent and have control. We had to become an extension of her and support her, not take over. Very little is negotiable in Mrs. F's schedule these days. She's fully in charge of it, she's booked solid, and she's aging with fire.

CHAPTER SEVEN

The Voices of Angels: Reflections on Caregiving

I have learned that caregiving in the home is made up of many moving parts. On a macro level it requires operational discipline, attention to detail, and a range and assortment of skills. On the most significant level, caregiving requires a rare combination of passion, compassion, and acquired skills. One does not wake up one day and announce the intention to become a caregiver for a senior. Of this I am absolutely sure. There is a journey to caregiving that is as dignified and diverse as the caregivers who make it. While I strongly believe in the critical need for professional case management and strong business practices as an employer, I do know it is the aides that are the secret sauce in supporting an elder to age in place.

Unfortunately, we are experiencing a never-before-seen shortage of caregivers. Perhaps the time is right to encourage angels in our own personal networks to consider the gift of caregiving. Perhaps these unscripted reflections from five senior caregivers will inspire action so each of us can embrace our inner caregiver and encourage others.

10 Reflections

1. Caregivers aren't made, we are simply made that way.

"I had a grandmother in a nursing home. She had dementia and was badly treated by her family. I visited her and she gave me one of those 'something's not right' looks. If you've ever gotten one of these, you know what I mean. I decided that moment that I could not leave without her. That's when I knew I'd be a caregiver. I recognized my heart. I knew what I was called to do."

"I'm 68 now. Nine years ago I divorced and moved in with my 85-year old mother when she had early stages od dementia. I didn't technically know what dementia was, but I knew she shouldn't be left alone at home or cooking for herself anymore. That was when I found my purpose. It started with caring for her, but since then it has turned into my life's work. This is such important work – caretaking the elderly who have lived important lives. I have now acquired so many skills and so much knowledge about aging. I can't put a price tag on this. I now delight and find great peace in caring for a 99 and 100-year old couple."

2. We are built to listen and learn.

"You get incredibly close and intertwined in the lives of these seniors and their families in the most significant ways. You learn about their personal histories and, if

130

you're lucky, become an extraordinary extension of their life stories."

"I have gained so much wisdom from seniors. Their morals are amazing. I have come to respect their personal life stories. They make me wonder 'what will I be like when I am their age? How will I be treated?' We have to be guardians of the elderly. We have to protect and advocate for them because so many of them cannot advocate for themselves."

3. **We thrive in one-to-one relationships.**

"I tried working in an assisted living community and it was just not the same. It is so important to me to have a one-to-one relationship with my client. I'm simply not built to have too many people to care for, but just one very strong, very tight, and close (relationship)."

"We can take what we learn in these deep relationships and apply it to our own families, our own grandparents and relatives. We are all going to need each other as we get older and this work that I am doing now, at age 40, will be even more important as I grow older. Every day I am aware of something new in the life of my senior. No two days are the same, especially if you leave your heart open to change and finding joy in each other's company."

4. **We never take no as an answer.**

"I had a 70-year old client who had a reputation for being incredibly difficult. She was a long-time, big-time drinker, swore like a trooper, and was in hospice. She was all-around pretty miserable. When I arrived on the scene she was quiet, angry, and belligerent. Her answer to everything was 'no'. She refused to shower, get dressed, or go out. After a few days I finally got her in my car. We made trips to Castle Island and Dairy Queen. She was aching for swordfish, so off we went to buy a piece that I cooked for her. I delighted in *her* delight as she ate it. She beamed every time I walked through that door."

"My client at first refused to open the door for me. Once we got past that, he refused to open the door for ***everybody else***! The doorbell would ring and a visiting nurse would be outside waiting to change the dressing on his back. He would peek around at me and ask if it was OK to let her in. I would give him the nod that it was OK. It took me a long time to earn his trust but it was worth every second of effort."

5. **Our journeys have never defined us, but they have determined us.**

"I came here from Honduras. I started from zero. For a while I slept on a floor. I have worked several jobs at a time, including running a taxi company. Now, I am a US citizen. I have gone to school to improve my English. I'm working as a caregiver in a job where it is tough to find the words to describe what I do. I am blessed in this work. Even if the day is bad, I know I bring joy to the senior. Now I have my HHA (Home Health Aid) and CNA (Certified Nursing Assistant). I'm 43, and I am so determined to learn more. I have seen families put seniors into nursing homes and assisted livings when all they (the senior) want to do is to be at home. I understand and respect that. I honor their wishes because I understand how precious it is to have a voice in being at home."

6. **We come from different countries but have the same heart.**

"I was born in Jamaica and had my first child in high school. That pretty much changed my life, but it was what happened five years later that defined me. At 18, my grandmother had open heart surgery in New York and I came to the U.S. to personally care for her. I remember her whispering in my ear 'You were born for this.' And I was. I have never looked back. My step-mom is a VNA nurse, and I would make house calls with her and volunteer at the elder service center in Cambridge. I'm now applying to college to be a nurse. I'm won't be stopped in my passion to take care of seniors, especially those who are unable to speak for themselves."

7. **We can spot a kindred spirit in a subway car and in a supermarket line.**

"Caregiving is an easy job to 'get,' but is not a job for just anyone. I can spot a great caregiver a mile away, even over the phone, just by the questions they ask and how they ask them. You have to think of the senior in your care as your mother, your grandfather, your great aunt or uncle. These cannot be strangers you are caring for, but a part of your family. It may sound like a little distinction, but it is not. It's a very big thing. I can be in the market and see a senior with a caregiver. Right away I can see if they are 'clicking' or not. I can tell if they are *simpatico* or just a senior and a paid caregiver. You get very good at picking up on these vibes."

"I don't think you can 'sell' caregiving. You have to be created to do this. I can tell you to be this way and that way when you go into a senior's home, but you have to *be* compassionate, which is nothing that is taught. It just is. Yes, many 'caregiving skills' can be taught, but not compassion.

8. **This is not, nor will it ever be, about the money.**

"Do not *ever* do caregiving for the money. Don't even think about it that way. Do it for the *honor* of working with seniors. Do it for the joy in it. Do it to learn from these amazing elders who have lived extraordinary lives. If you think about caregiving for money, you are doing it for all the wrong reasons."

"I had a client who had stopped talking altogether. He refused to talk to any caregiver that came into his home. He refused to take a shower. From what I had learned from my training he had dementia. But I surprised him, his family, even myself. After several visits, I asked about the radio and CD player that sat on the kitchen counter, unused. Well, before long I had him singing the words to his favorite old songs and I got him into that shower dancing!"

9. We cannot imagine any other "work."

"I used to have jobs in the corporate world; administrative jobs and such where I knew I was making a contribution, working on teams, and fulfilling what I thought to be important tasks. But there is no job like this one, where at the end of the day you feel you've made such an incredible difference in someone's life."

"If you are fortunate enough to connect with a family for a few years, you have created a relationship and bond of epic proportion. It's a treasure and gift in which you actually get back more than you give."

10. So, Why Do We Do This?

"My grandmother told me to, and I know she's in heaven keeping an eye out to make sure I am."

"Because I have this heart."

"Because every day I am totally surprised by my life. Who could ask for more?"

"I sleep better at night knowing that I did good today."

"Joy.....Just joy. I make a difference in someone's life and at the end of the day it simply gives me joy."

"Purpose. Taking care of people who have lived such important lives – even though they may not think so – gives me such a sense of purpose."

"There is a saying 'Once a man, twice a child'. We need to step up for those who can no longer step up and care for themselves. This is God's work."

"These are not jobs we do, but simply moments of good, bound together by other moments of good."

Thanks to Senior Helpers Caregivers: LG, JH, PR, JP, BM

CHAPTER EIGHT

Living with Complex, Complicated and Progressive Diagnoses

Home has become a growing and "in-demand" option for aging in place, even as seniors are challenged by complicated, chronic and complex medical issues. Home Care response is equally sophisticated in support, state of the art caregiver training, and case-driven approach to care.

This is the new era of personalized Home Care. We are never surprised and you are never alone.

Confronting the Audacity of Dementia: Weaving Comfort & Care at Home

As I started to write this, I became skeptical about its contents. I am all too familiar with the statistics around Alzheimer's and dementia as we continue to fight to find a cure, increase our hope for prevention, and strive to reach for better outcomes. You probably know or knew someone with a form of dementia, such as Alzheimer's, or maybe you were or are currently caregiving for a loved one with this formidable disease.

I have seen what a diagnosis can do to a family. An Alzheimer's diagnosis, both for the individual affected and their surrounding Circle-of-Care has the potential to whip up every part of normal life, putting unexpected strains on finances and relationships. While we learn more about Alzheimer's all the time, there is still so much more we do not know about this disease. It's the "not knowing" part that is so unsettling because no two seniors present their disease the same way, each is different. While we are gaining new understanding about this disease we know one thing; it is a progressive disease for which there is no medical intervention that can materially impact the timeline or the outcome. Yet, there is much we can do to confront and comfort along the way. It is a medical diagnosis but it is largely a behavioral intervention. Care in the home is a powerful tool for families.

There are good reasons for this:

"Home" is becoming a resilient place for this journey. For many it is safer and can be customized and controlled, especially when buoyed with an essential Circle-of-Care standing at the ready. Furthermore, it is a familiar environment for the person affected. This is critical when the ability to form new memories is compromised or not possible. There are significant advances in managing the characteristics of this disease and its impact at all stages. More sophisticated and impactful approaches in caregiving are emerging all the time.

Plans Need Weaving, Positive Thinking and Flexibility

When we talk with families about customized care for dementia, I think of it as a strategy session. It is usually the first of many conversations we will have around managing the success (and potential failure) of a loved one through the stages of this disease. Each plan must name, engage, and involve a broad Circle-of-Care which includes essential providers and relationships that may weave in and out throughout the journey. When a family decides to caregive a loved one, we often recommend adding an Aging Life Care Advocate (GCM) to their "circle," someone who can suggest options along the way, as well as serve as a clinical and psychological resource for the individual and the family caregiver.

The Plan of Care must be approached positively and considered a moving target. At home, loved ones can safely thrive at each stage of Alzheimer's by keeping their world as large as possible and maximizing their engagement in it by understanding both limitations and possibilities.

A positive physical approach to caregiving has been inculcated in our general philosophy and culture through our Senior Gems® program developed for us by Teepa Snow. The Alzheimer's Association has created three major stages of Alzheimer's, while our Senior Gems® program identifies six. This granularity of perspective gives us subtle insight into changing social behaviors and physical and cognitive abilities so we can focus on what is possible and what can be done. We keenly understand the power of visual and verbal touches, cues, direct and indirect, and the potency of greetings, gestures, public spaces, habits, routines, and boundaries. Today, each of our caregivers has rigorous skills training in Alzheimer's and dementia. Proficiencies are constantly updated.

This valuable education is also offered to families and family caregivers. They, more than anyone else, are on the front lines with loved ones. Who better to understand the nuance of memory loss or a shift in attitude, behavior, verbal and visual acuity than a husband, wife or adult child living fulltime with a loved one? Who needs tools and tips more than a family caregiver, especially one on the scene every day, when it comes to providing reassurance, respect and positive feedback to a loved one with dementia? Because no two people journey through this disease the same way, days can be unpredictable and disruptive, and every care plan needs to be agile and flexible. This is also why family caregivers need a break from caregiving.

For family caregivers, "Adult Day Centers" are now providing respite; opportunities for their loved one to engage safely outside the home in programs and social activities alongside others with dementia. Seniors are supervised by trained caregivers and social service providers. Beehives of activities provide happy, positive and productive environments and win-wins for families.

As the disease progresses, the Plan of Care is destined to change, but not the strategy woven behind it. With ours, each is built on an ongoing assessment of potential roadblocks and a plan which continually works to mitigate potential risks for each of the seniors at every stage of Alzheimer's and dementia. We do not wait to hear that "Dad is having trouble eating" or "Mom needs help with the shower," because nurse-supervised visits and a review of the care logs will have indicated so. At the first sign of potential wandering, we understand immediately what options to recommend. We recognize the signs of family caregiver burnout because our Burden of Care assessment has already alerted us to this possibility.

Let Optimism Abound

In May of 2019, Mark Singer penned "Hello, Darkness," a story in *The New Yorker* about the legendary David Milch, noted Yale Professor and creator of hit TV shows like *Hill Street Blues, NYPD Blue* and HBO's *Deadwood.* Now at home in a converted garage he lives and works with advanced Alzheimer's.

Guided, supported, and uniquely understood by a tight circle of loved ones and friends, Milch continues to create, saying "I allow myself a provisional optimism about the possibilities of what time I will be allowed. And I permit myself a belief that there is possibly for me a genuine happiness and fulfillment in my family and in the work I do." It seems his Circle-of-Care has enabled Milch to gratefully confront the audacity of

Alzheimer's. If these complicated and sometimes complex journeys are to be made at home, optimistic plans can be woven, which can work wonders.

The Call for Exceptionalism

Why Parkinson's Care Demands Bold, Better, Now

When Michael J. Fox was diagnosed with Parkinson's more than 30 years ago, he explained he had two things to reckon with: "You deal with the condition, and you deal with people's perception of the condition."

"The Kid is Alright" is a powerful book that looks at how Fox has exercised, paced, accepted, humored, optimized, and vocalized his way through these last decades. The reason his story resonates is because it was, and continues to be, a family affair. My company cares for the "Michael J. Fox's" of the world every day.

When meeting a senior with Parkinson's we understand fully the responsibility to engage loved ones with important knowledge, while at the same time delivering caregiving with exceptional skills, deft hands and comforting hearts. When families first hear a Parkinson's diagnosis, they are often in a state of shock. They have now come face to face with the four Big "M's" that still underscore this disease; Misunderstood, Misdiagnosed, Mistreated, and Mismanaged.

Parkinson's is *Misunderstood.* *A* masked or expressionless face may have been taken as a sign of being depressed, angry, sad or, worse yet, onset dementia, when it may in fact have been the presence of this complex disease. A firm diagnosis can be okay.

Parkinson's is very often *Misdiagnosed.* There is no blood test, MRI, or x-ray currently available to diagnose Parkinson's, which is why it is so easily misdiagnosed, or people can go for years being treated incorrectly. It is a disease that progresses slowly, and contrary to popular belief, a person can have Parkinson's and not have any tremors.

Parkinson's is *Mistreated.* If seniors do not take their medications on time or eat the right food at the right intervals, it can result in serious consequences and hospitalizations. Medications, when taken early and with consistency have proven incredibly successful. Those affected can live for decades with the right therapies and with minimal disruption in their life.

Parkinson's is *Mismanaged.* Despite the wealth of information available from highly qualified and accessible sources, this disease appears in complex and highly individualized ways during its progression. Today's front-line treatments embrace a nuanced mix of medications, physical, occupational and speech therapies, amazing exercise programs, proven diet regimes, and sometimes surgery. Synergy can be met with amazing success.

No two people present Parkinson's exactly the same, and this is why the approach Senior Helpers has developed for caring for seniors with this diagnosis is exceptionally individual, flexible, and nimble.

A Patient Centered Care Management Plan, its philosophy and its approach, are the reasons why the Michael J. Fox Foundation selected Senior Helpers as its partner in providing Home Care for Parkinson's. We have a disease-centric approach to caregiving, and we understand that Parkinson's affects the whole family.

A Team Approach Works and Wins

A Care Plan is unique to each senior and each diagnosis within each family. It is nurse-driven and nurse-supervised. It is essential that a Parkinson's Plan identifies and helps the family integrate the critical players involved in the wellbeing of the senior; from dieticians, support groups and key neurologists, to every extended family member, primary care physician, therapists and work-out gurus. They are the ongoing support team and part of the balancing act in providing care and support for those with Parkinson's.

A professional in the Boston area with a personal Parkinsin's Disease journey stated: "With a Parkinson's diagnosis, I have seen families struggling to understand the complexity of symptoms they are seeing in a parent or loved one. They are anxious about how to maintain the status quo, and exactly what to expect next. Having a Care Management Plan gives them a sense of control over what is inherently unpredictable. The plan may change, but the goal is always the same. Keep the lines of communication open, and the network of support close at hand. This is a significant feeling of safety and security for a family."

Specialized Training Essential to Great Care

Our caregivers must be specifically trained prior to being assigned to Parkinson's families, because we understand that seeking professional care can be a game changer. Home Care has proven to lower risk of complications, extend life-expectancy and enhance the overall quality of life. This is also why our assigned caregivers are individually trained in Parkinson's care on a client-specific basis. Their learning includes in-depth understanding of cardinal motor and non-motor symptoms, tremors, rigidity, Bradykinesia, and the five stages and progression of the disease. They understand why noticing even slight changes in a senior's sense of smell, taste, voice volume and pronunciation is important, and they are equipped with a keen sense and urgency for timelines and routines.

Our Parkinson's Caregivers are skilled on the specifics required of a senior's exercise regime because it may lead to increased strength, improved balance and walking, and prevent falls. They are imbued with the importance of eating the right foods at the appropriate intervals, and the absolute demands of medication management.

As an industry professional recently noted, "I have a loved one with Parkinson's and professionally and personally I have tried to gain as much knowledge and insight as possible about this incredibly complicated diagnosis. There are so many moving parts [to Parkinson's], and it's much more than tremors. It is tremendously reassuring to know there are specifically trained and skilled resources in caregiving, such as cutting-edge exercise programs like Rock Steady Boxing, specialized support from the Parkinson's community, exciting clinical trials, and emerging services that are aligned and becoming more available at home. We are making exceptional strides."

Parkinson's affects about one million Americans, with about 60,000 diagnosed each year. The disease has no bias for race or socioeconomic group and by 2030 the number of people with Parkinson's is expected to double. There is no cure, but there is great need for an exceptional approach to care for those with this complex, confounding, and complicated disease. There is also an exceptional need to empower families with knowledge and confidence. So they, too, can impact the lives of loved ones. Although April is Parkinson's Awareness Month, let us be exceptional in our approach to providing better and bolder care for seniors and families every month.

We recognize needs beyond dementia and Parkinson's, including caregiving for traumatic brain injury, quadriplegia or other extreme physical limitations. We understand these complex medication routines are all part of this. Dementia is the largest of the progressive conditions and physical limitations are often what traditionally makes home a difficult solution. But as illustrated in our Chapter titled "Seven Journeys," our caregiving expertise and skills training are expansive, and we have rarely seen a case for which we have been unable to provide the "above and beyond" levels of care and compassion required.

When investigating agencies, ask about types of care they provide. Get references and example of needs similar to yours.

CHAPTER NINE

When Navigating the Most Important Journey of All

There is a time when the most important journey in life requires the family to leave caregiving and medicine reminders to others and simply be daughters, sons, partners, friends and loved ones. We understand that the end-of-life journey requires superior understanding and seamless care and support. Hospice is often shrouded in myth and misunderstanding and it is one of the most powerful and potent journeys we make. Here is a way you might think about it.

When Navigating the Most Important Journey of All, the Combination of Personal Support and Hospice Matters

While I do not have the opportunity to meet all of our clients, I do know something about each. With a nurse led and case-centered approach to caregiving, every client in our care has a full case file of what we do for them every day. This is true regardless of the scope of care, be it something as simple as transportation and accompaniment to medical appointments or complex physical care for an advanced Parkinson's diagnosis.

To ensure we provide the right care, at the right time by the right caregiver, it is the agency's job and that of the case managers to stay up to date on what is going on in the wider world of "caregiving." As you can imagine, it's a broad and deep field, and changing all the time. New therapies are being developed in helping care for Alzheimer's, and strategies for a successful "coming home" and recovery from acute care and the advancements in technology that are becoming more relevant. We also must manage the training and skill sets of our caregivers in order to ensure current expertise across a wide range of specialties.

End-of-Life Care is one of these areas where understanding the continuum of care and caregiver training are so very critical. While End-of-Life Care is one of the most precious forms of caregiving, one aspect of it seems to be cloaked in myth and misunderstanding: Hospice. Hospice care is complicated emotionally and "transactionally." I believe it is among the most precious forms of caregiving we provide to our seniors, families and loved ones. Hospice is often misunderstood because medical and other professionals are unprepared to talk about it. Our medical environment is a crush of multi-tasking and finding the right time to properly present the concept of hospice to families can be difficult.

Atul Gawande followed up his landmark *Being Mortal* with a documentary film about end of life. Promoted on *PBS Frontline*, the film posed five questions to ask that would allow everyone to understand what is truly important when facing their own mortality. Riveting in their simplicity, Gawande offers bold insights for bringing families and loved ones together during tender times.

Dr. Steve Landers, in his piece "Repeat After Me: Hospice Means More Care, Not Less," openly acknowledges that the profession falls short in giving hospice its due. As he puts it, "For us insiders, we have come to understand hospice is not about death. It is a practical and tangible way to live life to its fullest with dignity and comfort, more connected to family, friends and faith, more intentionally about one's legacy."

Seniors want to stay at home through the end. Home Care Agencies help them do this by recruiting and training the best caregivers, and giving them expertise to provide the seniors in our care with a superior experience. As an example, a select group of our caregivers are specifically trained in End-of-Life Care and how to work with hospice providers. Why? Because we understand this kind of care should be profoundly personal. We also know that it is highly specialized and requires a particular set of skills and backgrounds that must effortlessly coordinate our care plans with family needs and other care providers to provide seamless End-of-Life support for loved ones and family members in our care.

We are constantly reminded that families who experience hospice for the first time are surprised to realize that hospice services provide an entire team of supportive services and are a reimbursable benefit, free to the patient and available to those that meet the criteria.

As a member of all the communities we serve, we interact and serve side by side with many local hospices providers, and stand in awe at the innovation of the breadth of medical and non-medical interventions they bring to each individual. From music therapy and spiritual counseling, to empathic listening and readings and other deeply personalized counseling, we have witnessed first-hand the power of hospice to enable unique connections and comfort to families and loved ones in this emotionally laden time.

Like one of our hospice partners we share the sentiment that "Families who have used [hospice] services marvel at what a difference it provides for [their] loved one. Hospice is so supportive to the entire family coping with the inevitability of losing a beloved member of their family. Patients and families hesitating and waiting too long rather than being open to activating hospice services sooner is one of the biggest misconceptions of our services."

A Time to Simply "Be" Family

I have seen many seniors begin hospice along with support and I find myself sharing these thoughts with family and loved ones. I urge them to stop being caregivers, cooks, drivers to endless medical appointments, and medicine "reminders." I urge them to let hospice provide the medical and holistic support, and Home Care provide the personal care needs so they may simply be sons, daughters, husbands, wives, granddaughters, brothers, sisters, friends and partners.

Life with the combination of Home Care and Hospice care can be a life filled with intention, where seniors feel more alive and more human than their illness or condition has perhaps allowed them to be in months, or even years. I always encourage families to share this incredible time with each other through photographs, story-telling, or just being in each other's presence. It is here that hospice can create rarified connections and space for immense, undiluted caring.

If you are navigating End-of-Life Care, I hope you find these thoughts helpful. For Home Care Agencies the role as caregivers is always very clear. We are here for you, your families and your loved ones whether serving your needs alone or with our partners in care, there is certainly no myth or misconception about that. If this is the time you are navigating, speak to them about their philosophy of care at end of life. Discuss your goals and the role you need them to play. At such precious times, a one-size-fits-all approach to care won't work. It has to be individualized and flexible. They also must have experience. The role of a nurse inside the agency for case management is critical. There are many clinical needs that have to be defined and coordinated at end of life between the hospice and other clinical providers. The nurse in the Home Care Agency is critical for ensuring these needs are translated into the care plan and that this be done continuously as these needs change on a near daily basis.

CHAPTER TEN

Going it Alone: Implications and Optimism

For millions of seniors, adult children serve as full time "underground" caregivers; many of whom consider themselves "alone", stressed out and making difficult choices every day about the care of a loved one. The fact is, the number of seniors being supported with a patchwork of care is growing. Some of it works very well, and some not so well.

This book has been dedicated so your journey of aging and those of a loved one are as good as they can be. You are not alone, and we hope we've empowered you with information to make thoughtful and prudent decisions. With planning and optimism, your best days as a caregiver are ahead of you.

"Going it Alone" is Not the Same as Being Alone

In September 2018, *The Boston Globe* published an article by Linda Matchan titled "Stranger in the House." Upon reading it, I was torn between great sadness, outrage and considerable frustration. Her article seemed to summarize so many challenges of individuals trying to navigate care for a loved one under the well-intentioned but clearly false belief they knew "what good looked like." That they knew what was important when it came to care, and that they knew how to select providers.

As the story unfolds, you truly feel for the woman at the center of it; for her experience and how poorly it played out. It could have been entirely avoided with a little research, a little support and by not trying to take short cuts.

What follows is extracted from my response to the article. If you would like to read the article you can Google "Stranger in the House" Boston Globe, September 2018. (subscription required). And to view my formal response, you can visit www.guide4aging.com/bosglobe My response was not published. I did, however, have an exchange with Ms. Matchan. This is a case study in what can go wrong, but more importantly it is a series of lessons learned for all of us. Ms. Matchan describes stories in which families, in desperate need of care for frail, disabled, and aging loved ones at home, fall victim to physical abuse, theft and worse by home health aides and personal care attendants they assumed and trusted to be honest and well-meaning. Instead of being properly vetted and credentialed to work, these hired "caregivers" took advantage of clients by swindling life savings, stealing medications, and exploiting handicapped elders.

Two articles in *The New York Times* also stuck with me lately. Thematically, they don't seem to mesh. But when conflated, they paint a similar picture. The first, entitled, "We Need Each Other: Seniors are Drawn to New Housing Arrangements", speaks to a decade long rise in the phenomenon of seniors finding each other and developing natural communities of co-habitation. These can be through matchmaking programs like that operated by the New York Foundation for Senior Citizens, the national Village to Village movement, or looser constructs using communities connected through emails, and Facebook. The point being, pragmatic and increasingly efficient seniors are foregoing traditional nursing homes, independent and assisted living and seeking each other out to create their own, fundamentally better housing and care alternatives.

The second piece, "Why Aren't More Women Working? They're Caring for Parents," reveals the trials of a massive and somewhat silent labor force. These are the millions caring for elders who are also holding down full-time jobs and where leaving the labor force is not an option. These caregivers, mostly women, forgo at least $28.9 billion per year in wages when they take time off to care for children or sick relatives. These family caregivers are professional jugglers and emergency room warriors. They pay close attention to the cost of everything, and put off their own emotional and physical requirements for the needs of a parent, grandparent or loved one.

Though both of these groups of seniors seem different on the surface, just below you will find elders and caregivers who are, in effect, "going it alone." They are outside of the mainstream of what we think of as traditional caregiving settings for a host of reasons. Seniors are living longer than expected, families are mobile and adult children are spread out globally. Therefore, health care policies and medical leaves have been unable to keep up with the realities of the times, and company benefits differ wildly. The list goes on. *"Going it alone" is not the same as being alone.*

Still, the notion of "going it alone" does not have to mean "being alone" when it is time to make important decisions about getting care and caregiving. In both of these settings, the world of caring for a senior loved one or taking care of each other is incredibly complex. It is a collision of personal needs, individual desires, and changing conditions with a new break down of player roles. It is a constantly shifting model of care driven by insurance and Medicare/Medicaid disrupting the healthcare continuum; clashing with multi-generational demographic shifts, myths, facts, lions and tigers and bears – Oh My!

The first step is to understand you are not alone. Millions are going through what you are. Let's step back and look at figures compiled by the Family Caregiver Alliance regarding work and caregiving. Millions of family and unpaid caregivers assist 7.7 million community-dwelling older adults with daily activities: more than one in six Americans are working full-time or part-time assisting with the care of elderly family members, relatives or friends. In addition, 70% suffer work-related difficulties due to their dual roles, and 69% report having to rearrange work schedules, decrease hours, or take unpaid leaves to meet caregiving responsibilities. Finally, 61% experience at least one change in their employment (warnings, negative performance reviews, forced early retirement, loss of job benefits), while single females caring for elderly parents are 2.5 times more likely than non-caregivers to live in poverty in old age.

If you are "going it alone" in either of the scenarios described in *The New York Times,* you already know days can be challenging both emotionally and physically. You have recognized the impact caregiving has had on you professionally, emotionally, and personally, and the tradeoffs you have made along the way.

While these statistics provide a backdrop, they fail to tell the stories we typically see every week in Home Care Agencies.

First story: Every week we meet adult working children who are providing or orchestrating daily support for mom or dad. Things are ok at first; going to doctor's appointments, getting prescriptions filled, etc. It is the cumulative impact that tells the story. Less time with family, a missed promotion, cancelled vacations. This is the story of good intent but flawed execution and unforeseen outcomes. This is exactly the story Ms. Matchan describes in her *Boston Globe* article.

Second story: This is when a crisis hits; something happens, a fall, an illness, an acute medical episode (heart attack) or a chronic medical condition takes an abrupt turn. Things change in an instant and decisions have to be made fast.

In both of these situations the result is the same. Help is needed, but what kind? How to figure it out, how to navigate it and how to achieve the outcomes you need for success for yourself or your loved one.

Distinguishing Support: Medical, Navigational, Direct

If you are "going it alone," even in a crisis situation, you can still stay in control and make good decisions; and do so in a way that allows you to course correct as needed. If Medical Support is required you know right away to call 911 and get to an emergency room or urgent care. If broader Navigational Support is required, there are many options you have for short, medium and long-term advice; which may begin connecting with your nurse practitioner or elder care resources available through your council on aging. Your state Aging Life Care Association can help match you with an appropriate geriatric care manager.

Direct Support for critical hands-on care, respite, companionship and support for dementia, Parkinson's and recovery care are provided by home care agencies. They help you customize and strategically course correct for both short, medium and longer term.

This is my point: It is important to sort out expertise versus experience, to sort out what, by whom, when and how much support is required. In spite of being in a crisis, you can ask questions that provide critical perspectives to reducing rather than increasing risk to you or your loved one's life.

Taken collectively, the articles in *The Boston Globe*, and *New York Times* all reverberate because they confirm that millions of seniors (or their primary caregiver), in differing living configurations, are "going it alone." This does not mean, however, they *are* alone. They have the same arsenal to fall back on if they assess honestly, plan, prioritize, and are willing to course correct. To pick up on Ms. Matchan's article, here is the detailed response of why things could have gone differently.

With No Licensing, Definitions of "Home Care" Differ Widely

Because there are no standards or certifications required for starting a Home Care company in Massachusetts (and over 15 states in the US,) variations of "Home Care" differ widely. As the *Globe* article clearly proves, the definition of a "qualified" caregiver or aide can border on obscene. Check if your state has defined licensing standards and take the time to understand what those licensing standards are and mean relative to:

- Who can provide care
- Employment versus contractor models
- Who manages care (nurse, social worker etc.) and what frequency case management must be performed
- Background check requirements and what those requirements mean
- Insurance and other protection requirements

More players in Home Care has meant more business models, including private hire agencies, registries, and of course the merry-go-round of aides-for-hire found in the Yellow Pages, and on Google, Care.com, Craigslist and others. Most of the families in *The Boston Globe* article went outside the box, hiring (in good faith) on their own and were completely unprepared to deal with what and who arrived in their homes.

Ms. Matchan's heartbreaking article makes many points through several examples, but the case and critical need for qualified professional caregiving agencies and caregivers are both clear. With the growing complexities of Alzheimer's, dementia, ALS, and Parkinson's diagnoses, there must be specific, specialized and dedicated caregivers; always learning essential skills and leaning in for loved ones.

The Dangers of Hiring Caregivers Directly Because of Perceived "Cost Savings"

I understand that families often feel an agency's services are "too expensive" and seek to replicate what agencies do on their own. *The Boston Globe* article speaks to the perils inherent in this. The difference in cost between hiring an agency and hiring a caregiver privately is the cost of managing the significant variables that largely prevent the tragic situations presented here.

What do "Costs" of Home Care Really Represent?

While there is a void of regulation in Massachusetts, franchise brands like ours, Senior Helpers, or caring independent agency providers, do it right, and are true partners in care with the families and individuals they serve. They invest in things that protect you and make a difference in the care they provide. What do those investments represent? I can only speak to my own agency, which includes the following costs:

- HR Processes: Our comprehensive Hiring and Skills Verification Process screens our caregivers and reference checks them. They then undergo a national criminal and sexual offender background check along with a national motor vehicle check on an annual basis.
- Caregiver Training: Our system standards require multiple hours of dementia training, hands on general care instruction and case specific training. We have full training rooms for review and training in the Activities of Daily Living (ADLs) and even a full Home Health Aide training program taught by a Registered Nurse. We also insist on Home Health Aide or Certified Nursing Assistant certification to provide hands on care.
- Nurse Intake: Our skilled nurses meet with our clients prior to beginning service, document status and craft an individual care plan as an instruction tool for the aide(s) involved. They also often provide the case specific training required for our client's success.
- Caregiver Bench Strength: It is more than just finding a caregiver. It is about finding a caregiver that meets the need of "fit" and "skills" to support the client's success. Clients and caregivers are people, so personality matters. This is a soft science, but critical to care success.

Additionally, caregiver replacement in times of sickness, a change in need etc. are critical needs. In short, our clients do not miss care because of a call out. We have trained caregivers to meet with the daily challenges of being an employer.

- Nurse Case Management: Our nurses make ongoing visits to validate status, update care plans, review case documentation and work with our families as their partner on the journey of aging.

- Respect for the state and federal wage and hour laws (wage rates, tracking hours, breaks, paying overtime, providing sick time with compensation.) It is far more than just using a payroll company for distribution of wages, it is also making sure those wages are appropriately calculated and the paycheck stub laws are held and it is a proper working environment for our most special employees – our caregivers.

- Insurance: Comprehensive liability protection that ensures the resources are there if, in the rare occasion, something does happen. Workers' compensation and unemployment insurance protects our aides and you.

- Satisfaction Guarantee: This provides our clients the open door to discuss their care and enables us to respond to care good or bad and address issues immediately.

My agency has advised families on how to hire privately. This is where the sadness is felt. There are ways to do it successfully. Had someone explained the details of what a reputable agency does and what it takes to replicate the risks we take on and manage, most find agency costs are both fair and reasonable.

Why We Advocate for Change

The alternative to hiring a well-run agency is what is detailed in Ms. Matchan's article: high risk and bad outcomes. This is why I strongly advocate licensure in my state for Home Care companies. What is about to happen with Medicare Advantage Plans is an example unfolding across the country. That is, insurance companies are slowly accepting that services provided by home care agencies are necessary to successful outcomes for our most vulnerable elders. This is good for seniors and good for business, because successful outcomes will be cost effective by reducing hospitalizations and other critical care occurrences.

My agency actively participated in the formation of the Home Care Association of America in Massachusetts, which is accredited by the Home Care Alliance of Massachusetts and is also a member of other related state associations. These are the associations in the state looking out for both families and providers in Home Care – not the state itself. We are staunch proponents of consumer protection, which licensure would achieve, and have voluntarily set the bar and standards for our own businesses extremely high.

In a rapidly changing discharge landscape where individuals spend less time in rehab and more recovery is expected to be accomplished at home, it is no longer appropriate to expect caregivers to come from a neighborly referral or Google search. It must be accomplished with surgical precision and attention to details such as: caregiver training and certification, specialized nurse and supervisor oversight, customized plans, hiring criteria, company liability, and a Client Bill of Rights. This is just for starters.

Families Have Too Much to Lose. They Must Be Smart in Asking the Right Questions.

If a private agency is not an affordable option, and a family decides to hire caregivers privately, it must do so intelligently, legally and with eyes wide open. Otherwise, that family stands to suffer the outrageous and egregious examples of caregiver malfeasance reported in this *Globe* article, in addition to being ill-prepared for potentially lethal employment claims where families are at risk of losing everything financially – and this happens!

The issue of asking questions, gathering data, and getting smart goes beyond Home Care, however. It goes to all medical providers who touch seniors and families. In today's healthcare we are bombarded by too many choices at discharge, and given too many options when we are in crisis. It's imperative that we all step back, take a deep breath, compare and research. I am often bewildered to find consumers research their new flat screen TV options with more precision than they do the agencies the discharge planner is recommending, or the rehab facility in which they're scheduled to spend the next two weeks. Real data exists on facilities when we are planning surgery, looking for a new specialist, or considering a move to long-term care. Platforms like "hospital compare," "doctor compare" and "nursing home compare" are available resources to help us execute our right of choice; we should never assume there is only one way of approaching our care.

Families need to study these sites, understand the information and know where referrals actually come from. We are living in times where physicians are not always right because they are overwhelmed and stressed. In hospitals, we are often seen by rotating surgeons, MD's of various titles, and a sea of faces with no personal history of us as individuals. Removed from the familiarity of our primary care physician, it behooves all of us to stop, study up, and ask questions.

In today's healthcare system, elders have a choice. Discharge planners who are setting up rehab and home health are obligated to provide you with options. Expect them and demand them. Because of today's Accountable Care Organization (ACO), elders will get recommendations for care within the network. It is now more important than ever to raise a voice if the care received is ill-advised or mismatched. It happens, but it takes your voice to make a change.

The more you know, the more control you have over the management of your care. It sounds obvious and simple, but it takes energy, commitment and courage to stay on top of your own care by "looking under the hood" and asking the right questions. In a world where more seniors are deciding to age in place at home, the mandate for loved ones is choosing reputable, philosophically grounded, experienced and caring providers. Navigating elder care is complicated, and the current and projected ongoing labor shortage makes it more so. Even finding a reputable agency can be difficult, because most assume all are the same and often seek to compare only on price. How any one agency conducts itself, its method of managing the seven core needs identified above, may be far different from how another agency does the same, if they do it at all. Our hope for our clients and the Commonwealth at large is that families learn the right questions to ask and most importantly, understand the right answers.

Lastly, and as important as the quality of the agency I own and run, is the fact that I am local. I and my employees live and work in the communities we serve. We attend churches and synagogues here, we educate (or educated) our children in the schools. The journeys of the seniors we shared in Chapter Six are very real to all of us here every day because in each of those elders was a glimpse of one of our grandmothers, uncles, aunts, neighbors or dads. You just don't get any more personal than this when you show up to care.

My point of sharing this as the ending of the book is not to scare but to empower you. My message is this: YOU CAN DO THIS! Whether you are figuring out your plan, your next steps, your providers, your style of advocacy, intervening in a crisis or just managing day to day – YOU CAN DO THIS!

This book is written in hopes that your story does not reflect the outcomes of the seniors written about in *The Boston Globe* article.

CHAPTER ELEVEN

Conclusions and Glossary of Terms for Successful Aging

If I have empowered and informed your journey of aging, then I will have considered this book a success. What is left are some helpful checklists to keep you grounded and in control, a glossary of terms to help you understand the players, and a helpful list of Frequently Asked Questions. Your journey of aging is one of a kind and yours to take and make. Bold and safe travels!

My objective in compiling this book is to provide information and incentive; especially those hard-won lessons learned by playing a part in the journeys of seniors over the last decade. What follows are a few additional thoughts I hope you will find useful.

The first is a series of checklists I hope you find supportive as you move forward. The second is a glossary of terms to demystify the language we professionals so easily speak but sometimes rarely explain. Neither are perfect, nor a universal fit for every situation; but they will provide you with a starting point and some guardrails.

Do what you can, get support where you need it. Know that the Journey of Aging is a moving plan and you must be flexible in your ongoing support of it for yourself and your loved one.

Checklists for Success

Chapter One: Patience and Persistence make an honest assessment of your current Navigational Challenges and Assumptions.

- What is your current Health/Ability to function? (healthy active, health declining, chronic health/decreased mobility, declining chronic health/extreme decreased mobility, complete health decline/non-mobile)
- Where do you prefer to live?
- What costs have you anticipated for your care?
- What resources (public/private) do you believe are available? (private funds, family caregivers, social security, community services, VA Benefits, Medicare/Medicaid, etc.)
- If "Home" is not the Best Option: What are the current considerations? Define who should be in your "Circle-Of-Care". Why? (friends, family, professionals, medical/clinical support, neighbors, resources, consider their roles and why you include them)
- What is needed to manage safety, autonomy and independence, medical condition. Assess if it creates an acceptable Burden of Care on others.

Chapter Two: Becoming an Educated Consumer.

Make an honest profile and definition of your "Day".

- How do you describe a good/great day? (healthy active, time with friends, getting out in community, reading, exercise and outdoors, quiet and contemplative, etc.)
- What would you like to do differently if you could?
- What causes you stress and anxiety?
- Where would you most like to age?
- What resources do you believe are available to help you do so (private funds, family caregivers, social security, community services, VA Benefits, Medicare/Medicaid, etc.) ?
- Define who should be in your "Circle-Of-Care (friends, family, professionals, medical/clinical support, neighbors, etc.), and consider their roles and why you include them.
- What aspects of Patient Centered Care are most important to you and why?

Chapter Three: Prepare to Succeed

"The Conversation": If you are an adult child or family member caregiving a senior or loved one:

- How have you prepared for these important conversations?
- What is the overall plan for the conversation, and who will be involved?

- What outside resources are available to you down the road for support?
- What is the expanded circle of family support you can count on?
- What role will each of you play and how will decisions be made?
- How will you determine what next steps to take?
- If "Home" is not the Best Option: What are the current considerations?

Continue to define (and refine!) who should be in your "Circle-Of-Care". Why? Because now that you know the risks and concerns that need to be managed, you need to know who in your circle is best equipped to help you! (friends, family, professionals, medical/clinical support, neighbors, resources, consider their roles and why you include them) What is needed to manage safety, autonomy and independence, as well as medical condition and Burden of Care.

Chapter Four: Scoring for Success

This Chapter uses the LIFE Profile methodology to help manage risk at home through a structured plan of care and support. The LIFE Profile can be used as an independent assessment or in conjunction with a plan of customized support. A way to think about its value is to think about how you value plans to age in place at home, and what concerns you might have about doing so. The proprietary methodology is powerful, however the key for you is to understand its areas of focus and how it is used.

What safety risks do you worry about at home? Be specific about these, especially if you live alone or live with a spouse or loved one who may not be fully capable of supporting your safety risks. What concerns do you have about medication and general medical management? How would you honestly assess your independence and autonomy as you read this chapter? How would you honestly assess the burden of care you place on those around you because of your current physical or medical requirements? How would you honestly assess your engagement in life?

Back to your plan:

- How have you prepared for important conversations?
- Who will be involved?
- What outside resources are available to you down the road for support?
- What is the expanded circle of family support you can count on?
- What role will each of you play and how will decisions be made?
- How will you determine what next steps to take?
- If "Home" is not the Best Option: What are the current considerations?

Chapter Five: Home Care: What Really Matters and Why

If you are thinking of hiring a Home Care Agency for a loved one, or referring Home Care to a senior or family, consider the implications of this chapter:

- Ask how the agency will communicate with you and how you will have access to those managing and defining care.
- Ask how frequently a case manager will make house calls to discuss care, brief the primary contact, and inquire how things are going.
- Ask about the depth and range of caregiver expertise as well as specific experience around your support issues; how has the Home Care Agency approached situations like your own?
- Be sure to ask for current references that apply to a situation similar to yours.
- Understand clearly and definitively how your caregivers are trained, verified, and screened for your care. How do they communicate with each other around your care?
- Ask about how care plans are developed, written and communicated. How will your "great day" be decided?
- Ask about the agency's use of technology in the development of a plan of care, and the management of your plan specifically.
- Meet with the agency in person; ask questions, talk about how changing circumstances and how concerns are communicated and managed.

Chapter Eight: For Progressive and Chronic Conditions

It is important to understand exactly where your loved one is along these complex journeys and as needed over time.

Establish goals:

- Macro (Long Term) – e.g. Aging in place with complex and chronic diagnoses as they relate to modifications, level of care required, safety, burden upon family caregivers, participation in available programs, etc.
- Micro (Short Term) – e.g. These tend to be care specific or specific objectives for the week, month, etc.
- Determine specific requirements of caregiver training – both family and professional.
- Identify credible, professional sources of advice and your "Circle-of-Care."
- Think beyond the clinical/medical .
- Consider family education on the details of care and care techniques.
- Who will be able to help you navigate your journey to the extent it is feasible and appropriate?
- Develop a PLAN: for *When Home is Not the Best Place to Be.*

Chapter Ten: Going it Alone

Get a notebook and write down your questions: record the answers and who gave them to you.

Prioritize these issues. Here are five categories to help structure your thinking. Rank the line items under each and across each category:

- Medical Issues & Conditions (think in terms of reconciling medications, issues around getting meds, medication reminders, monitoring and reacting to vital sign changes)
- Safety Around the Home (think in terms of your environment – home, how tasks are completed, the real level of capability or trouble of your loved one to do things alone or with assistance)
- Autonomy and Independence (think of being able to do everyday things – ease of bathing, grooming, toileting, walking, getting food, eating, paying bills, getting to doctor's appointments)
- Caregiver Burdens (make a side by side set of calendars of your loved ones needs and yours – what are the gaps? what are the physical, financial or emotional limitations for the first two weeks, the first 90 days and then beyond?
- Engaged in Life (what are the needs, desires and wants of your loved one for a rich and full daily pattern of living?). Identify what needs are permanent and ongoing and what needs are likely to change for the better or

worse over the next 30, 60, 90-plus days.

Start by being honest – where do you have enough information or expertise? (It is not about experience) Where do you not? Identify where you need more and where can you get it. Remember, you cannot always "check all the boxes." Some needs and desires cannot be met or should not be met. That is OK. Successful aging, wherever it is taking place, is a balancing act on a moving platform!

GLOSSARY OF TERMS

Activities of Daily Living (ADL)

The activities that fall into this category basically involve all tasks that are needed to be performed in order for the patient to survive comfortably. It is often provided by non-medical staff (usually a Certified Nursing Assistant) from an in-Home Care Agency.

Mobility

Many advanced patients often have problems with mobility. Things like getting out of the bed, walking to the bathroom and walking to several rooms in the house can be very hard for an elderly person. An in-Home Care professional assists the individual especially if the loved ones are unable to provide the care required for the elderly.

Toilet and Bathing

Toilet needs are necessary. With the high risk for falls and slips, it is important to have someone assist senior patients when nature calls. However, it is important to take note that assisting them while using the toilet should be done with respect so that they still have dignity while being assisted. It is also important to install safety structures such as non-slip mats and bars to improve the safety inside the bathroom.

Personal Hygiene

Daily grooming is an important ADL that needs to be done regularly. This involves brushing teeth, wearing clean clothes, and basically maintaining cleanliness. An in-Home Care professional is adept not only at helping the elderly do these things, but also remaining careful with their feelings.

Feeding

People need to feed in order to survive, but some elderly patients are no longer capable of feeding themselves. People with dementia and Alzheimer's need assistance when it comes to feeding.

Instrumental Activities of Daily Living (IADL)

Activities that are under IADLs are specific types of ADLs. These activities are very instrumental in the life of a person, but do not necessarily involve personal activities such as those mentioned earlier.

Below are the types of that are considered IADLs.

Meal Preparation

It is important for the patient to eat nutritious and delicious food. An in-Home Care professional prepares food that can keep the person healthy, so that a patient doesn't rely too heavily on takeouts or deliveries.

Housekeeping

Light housekeeping is a very important IADL. An elderly person who is barely able to move is at a potentially high risk for hazards if they live in an unclean home. Thus, in-Home Care professionals can ensure that the home is clean and safe by taking active steps such as doing light cleaning and removing debris on the floor. The main purpose of doing light housekeeping is to prevent falls and other injuries caused by a messy house.

Transportation

Elderly patients have difficulty with mobility and their failing memories often make the simplest trips such as going to the doctor or grocery shopping impossible. In-Home Care professionals can provide help with making travel reservations or even drive the patient to where they need to go.

Both ADLs and IADLs are very important for seniors who have failing health and memories. They need assistance from people to perform tasks that are important for their survival. It is important that you consider getting the services of an in-Home Care professional near you.

SENIOR OPTIONS

What is Independent Living?

Independent Living communities are senior housing communities designed for independent seniors that desire the conveniences of community living. These communities offer a senior lifestyle filled with recreational, educational and social opportunities. Independent Living Communities may also be called "Retirement Communities," "Congregate Living" or "Senior Apartments."

What is a Memory Care Neighborhood

When a family member receives the diagnosis of Alzheimer's or a similar form of dementia or memory loss, the entire family is impacted. It is an emotionally and physically challenging disease for the senior and those who love them. In the earliest stages of the illness, an older adult might be able to remain in their own home or move in with a loved one who acts as a caregiver. As the conditions progress, however, safety, security, and quality of life might decline. Families often lack the time, skills, and knowledge to manage all the unique needs Alzheimer's disease or dementia creates. The senior's neurologist or primary care physician might suggest a family investigate Alzheimer's care options. This type of housing is typically referred to as memory care programs, these housing communities are designed to meet the challenges a person with dementia or Alzheimer's often faces.

What Is Assisted Living?

An assisted living community is the best of two worlds. It is a senior housing option that allows an older adult to maintain their independence while still having the assistance they need nearby. Assisted living communities are designed for adults who need help performing the activities of daily living. It might be assistance with bathing and grooming or a helping hand managing their medication schedule. Although communities have staff on-site 24 hours a day, the goal of assisted living is to keep residents as independent as possible. Every assisted living community has a unique personality and offers different levels of care, services, and amenities. Some are more upscale and formal, while others have a casual, relaxed environment.

What is an Adult Day Care Center?

Adult day care is a planned set of activities created to promote and encourage well-being through various health-related and social services. These centers often distribute well-balanced, nutritious meals with consideration of special diets as per request. Adult day care centers are open during the day, typically on a weekday schedule, involving capable staff in a clean, healthy and happy setting. Adult day care centers have different types of structures, they can be public, private or run in cooperation by both entities. An adult day care center serves to give caregivers a reprieve in their day to day care of the seniors they work for, giving them time to take care of other personal chores or deal with their own personal time as they see fit. They provide seniors the chance of activity, getting the chance to continue stimulating both mind and body.

What services are offered in Continuing Care Retirement Communities?

Continuing Care Retirement Communities (CCRC) are residential campuses that provide a continuum of care, from private units to assisted living and then skilled nursing care, all in one location. CCRCs are designed to offer active seniors an independent lifestyle from the privacy of their own home, but also include the availability of services in an assisted living environment and on-site intermediate or skilled nursing care if necessary.

What is Respite Care?

Respite Care is a temporary or short-term option for individuals. It could consist of in-Home Care or a short stay option in an independent, assisted, or skilled care community. It provides temporary relief from duties for caregivers, ranging from several hours to days. Taking care of an elderly person can be physically and emotionally exhausting. It's important for caregivers to seek out occasional relief from their responsibilities. Whether it's a few hours a week, or a few days or weeks a year for a vacation, respite care gives caregivers the ability to reduce stress, restore energy and maintain a balanced lifestyle. Some caregivers may want to try respite care to help gradually ease their loved ones into living at a senior housing community.

CHAPTER TWELVE

Care in a Crisis

Over the past three years, I have written extensively on the criticality of being informed and prepared. But when I started writing this book in 2019, there was no indication that around the beginning of March 2020 that a virus acting like influenza on steroids would travel around the world and like some terrible swift sword lay waste to our economy, our way of life, and the very act of "getting together." And now we are expected to stick together while keeping six feet apart.

Many have contacted me asking, "What do I do now?" "Is it too late to be prepared?" The answer is it is never too late to start to put plans in place. There is an immediate need to plan for the ongoing impact and disruption in our lives and of those entrusted to our care.

For Seniors this is a "Must do" versus a "Nice to do." The World Health Organization has extensively written on the roles and risks for the aging population in times of emergency. Loss of independence or even a loss of life have occurred way too often in many of the crises in the last decade. With the evidence from Italy and China, the impact of coronavirus on the elderly population will be even more significant.

Here are the 6 Critical Objectives for Orchestrating Care in a Crisis

1. Define basic needs

2. Be connected to the world at large

3. Maintain your lifelines to others / engage in Life

4. Create a safe and secure space

5. Document what is going on

6. Create a disaster plan and know when to implement

Define basic needs

Know your basic needs and your primary needs and devise a back up strategy for both. We recommend a focus on the following 13 areas.

Can you:

1. Get bills paid

2. Get groceries / household supplies

3. Have meals prepared

4. Get help if needed

5. Get laundry done

6. Take garbage out

7. Maintain clean food preparation space

8. Get house cleaned

9. Get transportation to necessary places

10. Use the phone

11. Have general mobility in the living environment and in places critical to visit

12. Get Activities of Daily Living (ADLs) met (e.g. bathing, grooming, toileting, ambulation, etc)

13. Manage your medical condition (get meds, dose meds, take as prescribed, manage vitals within defined parameters and escalate if needed.)

Be connected to the world at large

The importance of a plan B is paramount in times of disruption. For most, plan B and often Plan C, also known as "Uh oh, now what," relies on being able to quickly navigate many options on a moment's notice. Think about our reliance today on the internet to get things done. Whether a home-based connection or via a mobile phone or tablet, connectivity is a necessity in today's world. That said, many especially Seniors, do not have a sufficient connection.

Over the past two years, my home care agency and our franchisor have sought various technology-based care enhancements for our clients. Our goal was simple; can we provide a greater level of care or oversight at a lower cost through the use of technology to separate care? The results were quite surprising. While nearly everyone had smart (or smarter) phones and could text, Facetime or the equivalent, a surprising number (over half) did not have active internet service in their home. The challenges of our Covid19 day-to-day existence have clearly demonstrated internet access is a necessity.

Review the 13 basic needs above; how could you ensure these were adequately met without internet access? It would be possible, but it would also be difficult – particularly in times of mass need and disruption as we face today.

Maintain your lifelines / Engage in Life

Per AARP, "Social distancing shouldn't mean shutting out the world. We all need human connection, particularly in a crisis and especially with those who understand and care about us. Research has shown just how emotionally and physically harmful social isolation can be. Fortunately, we live in a miraculous age when we have a myriad of technological means — including telephone, email, texting, video chat and social media — to keep our friends and family members present in our lives. That may be the best available solace for all of us until this crisis passes."

Three types of needed lifeline connections

1. A responsible person who can escalate on your behalf: Set a specific person who you speak to each day at a specific time. Have a daily check in and give basic information so they can intervene if necessary or, if you fail to check in, know to call 911 on your behalf. The three areas we recommend are:

a. Your well being – BE HONEST about your ability to meet your 13 basic needs.

b. Your state as it relates to other needs that you are having trouble meeting

c. Changes they should be aware of (i.e., medication routines, appointments, etc.)

2. Connection to professionals you may need to access. Increasingly our medical professionals are communicating by dedicated websites or applications on our phones that allow us to communicate with them and for them to respond. The general ability to get a doctor or their staff, even in an emergency, is difficult and in a peak demand due to a crisis – likely impossible. These applications and sites ensure your doctor will get your message and can respond.

3. General connection to others: Stay connected to your friends and loved ones. Set call times up – make a plan. Set up a video chat or even a group one. These things are quite easy if someone shows you how. Email or social media is a great way to stay in touch and find out how things are going. AARP wrote: *"Share moments of mutual enjoyment and meaning"*. Even in a coronavirus confinement, upbeat instances still go some ways toward offsetting frictions both small and large. Put on the old movies or music that you always enjoyed together. Bring out the photo albums to remind you of wonderful vacations and family gatherings of the past. Make and savor the recipe that was always a family favorite. Sit together on the living room couch in silence holding hands.

(Note once again the importance of a reliable internet connection in maintaining lifelines especially in times of social distancing or sheltering in place.)

Create a safe and secure space that allows separation

I have written about the 144 potential safety risks in the home. Now is the time to minimize these risks. Not all of us or our environment has the full list but here is a way to think about it:

1. The Bathroom: Remove unnecessary clutter. Make sure non-slip tape is where it needs to be and that assistive devices are in place – grab bars. Make sure the things you need are in easy reach.

2. The Bedroom: Remove unnecessary clutter. Pick up loose items on the floor. Please consider removing things that could pose a fall risk. For example, loose throw rug or things that are hard to see in the dark.

3. The kitchen: Remove unnecessary clutter. Make sure basic kitchen / food prep needs are in reach so you can avoid the use of a stool to get things. Have food storage needs in place (Ziploc bags, resealable containers). It is recommended that staple canned goods are available - not hoarding quantities - but to have if needed.

4. Separation: If the size of your world has shrunk to the confines of your home, then it is crucial to figure out ways to carve out time and space that's still yours. Taking 20 minutes to go to a separate room from the person you're caring for or living with helps you clear your mind and recover a little. Even if you must be in the same room all the time, there may be ways to focus on your own needs. Read a book or listen to calming music with headphones as an example. There are many small ways to be present and available but also separate and self-contained.

Document what is going on

Remember when we were kids. Many kept a diary or a log of the most significant and or insignificant things going on. Keep a diary but keep it focused. Document how your day is, how you feel, who you spoke to. Capture what you are concerned about and who you should discuss it with. (Remember your daily calls – don't leave the important stuff out.). During times of chaos and stress, it is always best to have detailed notes to refer to rather than rely solely on memory. Document all these things so you have a good record.

Create a disaster plan

No matter where you live, have a disaster plan ready for you and those you care for.

Your plan should include a written list of current needs, routines and impairments. It should include all identifying information (date of birth, Social Security number and a current photo) as well as allergies, medications and diagnoses. Prepare a biography of your loved one that will better inform providers of their personality, interests and background. This is especially important for medical conditions where you or a loved one relies on others to be their "voice."

Consider where you could relocate in the event of need. Most importantly confirm its availability to you and how they can communicate if availability changes. Ensure they can meet your needs not just your shelter.

Thoughts

These are trying times. We are all managing stress, anxiety, uncertainty. When we have enforced round-the-clock together time it is easy for things to escalate. There are everyday frictions both small and large that all have the potential to escalate – resist the urge. I find myself saying I'm sorry a lot – it is sincere, even when I am not sure what I have done. I am sorry that I did something that caused stress on the other person. Don't beat yourself up, don't put down others.

Be kind to yourself, be kind to others. You never know what is going on in someone else's life, so let's all remember not to judge and most importantly to be kind. Viruses are contagious but so is bad attitude and aggression. But more importantly, so is kindness, empathy and support. Pay it forward, because you just don't know how the return can positively impact you or your loved one.

Let's all leave good footprints where we tread! And together we will weather the storm.

ACKNOWLEDGMENTS

Much like aging, writing this book has been a journey. It started as a quarterly letter to our clients, then grew to be the monthly editorial in the *South Shore Senior News* and an occasional interview on the "My Generation" radio show, where the hosts and editors of the paper, Patti Abbate and Tom Foye, would ask more detailed questions about one of the topics I wrote about. Patti put the bug in my ear that I should write a book. So, here we are!

Along the way, I was introduced to Cindy Connelly. Cindy began working with me to simplify and focus our company's marketing messages but then began helping me do the same with the monthly editorials. Her research and support brought great insight and relevance to the monthly editorial. Cindy helped me find my voice and my focus and for that I am truly grateful. This book would not exist without her support compiling the three years of writing. And an ongoing thank you to my editor, Steve White, without whom this book would never have crossed the finish line.

To my team at Senior Helpers – past and present - from whom I have learned so much. In particular, thank you to Robyn Shea. Robyn is an exceptional nurse, but more than that a thoughtful, caring, compassionate caregiver and leader in the business. The ability to think out loud with her helped me better understand the needs our seniors face and how we fulfill them.

My clients' journeys are each unique and from each of you – past and present, I have and continue to learn. My caregivers are amazing. As I wrote in the book, I came to realize even more how exceptional the people are. Their stories, their hearts and their passion for those they care for shows how one person's care and kindness can truly change another's life experience. The difference they make in our client's senior and often final years is a treasure to behold.

My inspiration and my grounding is my family. My in-laws, Steve and Barbara, have always been a source of advice and motivation. Their reflections on their journey have helped shape many aspects of this book.

To my Mom and Dad (Sue and Charles), the adorable couple whose photo grace the back cover of this book, your love, support and guidance are foundations in my life. Writing this book was and is about learning all I can to ensure your journey is the best it can be. Being part of your circle of care is a privilege and an honor!

Finally, to my wife, Carolyn, and my kids, Lee and Dora, you have inspired me to always want to make a difference. Thank you for enduring the worst of me as we walk together through life's twists and turns.

Made in the USA
Columbia, SC
30 April 2020